Twayne's English Authors Series

EDITOR OF THIS VOLUME

Herbert Sussman

Northeastern University

William Morris

TEAS 262

William Morris

WILLIAM MORRIS

By FREDERICK KIRCHHOFF

Indiana University—Purdue University at Fort Wayne

TWAYNE PUBLISHERS
A Division of G. K. Hall & Co.
Boston, Massachusetts, U. S. A.

Published in 1979 by Twayne Publishers,
A Division of G. K. Hall & Co.
All Rights Reserved

Printed on permanent/durable acid-free paper and bound
in the United States of America

First Printing

Frontispiece sketch of William Morris by Dante
Gabriel Rossetti courtesy of Birmingham
Museums and Art Gallery.

Library of Congress Cataloging in Publication Data

Kirchhoff, Frederick, 1942-
William Morris.

(Twayne's English authors series ; TEAS 262)
Bibliography: p. 176-79
Includes index.
1. Morris, William, 1834-1896—
Criticism and interpretation.
PR5084.K5   821'.8   78-31238
ISBN 0-8057-6723-1

For
Mary Love Thigpenn
and
Ruth Thigpenn Kirchhoff

Contents

About the Author

Born in Jacksonville, Florida in 1942, Frederick Kirchhoff received
A.B. and Ph.D. degrees from Harvard University and is currently
Associate Professor of English at Indiana University-Purdue University at Fort Wayne and Managing Editor of *CLIO: An Interdiscipli-
nary Journal of Literature, History and the Philosophy of History.* He
has published articles on John Ruskin and William Morris in various
journals and is now engaged in a study of nineteenth-century travel
writing.

Preface

William Morris was perhaps the most versatile genius of the Victorian Age. Recognized by his contemporaries as a major poet and more and more known in the twentieth century as the author of a remarkable sequence of prose romances, he was also an influential figure in the history of modern interior design and typography and a leading spirit in the development of British socialism. The format of this series has enabled me to write a book for which there has long been a need: a concise study of Morris' literary development. Paradoxically, most short books on Morris have attempted to cover the whole range of his achievement, while the authors of "big books" have focused on specialized areas of concern. I have, then, no qualms about offering a study that is limited in scope. Other than indicating the media in which he worked, I have omitted a detailed account of Morris' career as a designer and typographer. Similarly, I have examined his political thought only insofar as it appears in a literary context.

To those who believe Morris was primarily an artist or primarily a socialist, my approach may seem wantonly narrow. However, I would argue that narrowness is precisely what is called for. Doubtless there are affinities between Morris' wallpaper and fabric designs and his poetry, and the relevance of Marxism to the literary work of his last decade is incontrovertible. Yet his development as a writer is also—and, I believe, primarily—a literary phenomenon best understood by literary analysis. Morris' imaginative poetry and prose was not merely a reflection of his other interests or a vehicle for their dissemination: it was his central mode of self-discovery and expression. It is here, consequently, that we come closest to finding the man; it is here that any attempt to understand the inner significance of his work as a whole must begin.

I am grateful to my colleague George Dillon and my friends Sharon Dillon and Martin Fichman for their criticism and advice and to Sanford and Helen Berger for making their Morris collection available to me. Also, for their help and encouragement, I wish to thank Joseph Dunlap and Professors George Landow, U. C. Knoepflmacher, and Carole Silver.

Portions of chapter 2 appeared in *The Pre-Raphaelite Review* (1 [November 1977], 95–105); portions of chapter 4 in *Victorian Poetry* (15 [Winter 1977], 297–306) and in *Approaches to Victorian Autobiography* (ed. George Landow [Athens, Ohio: Ohio University Press, 1979], 292–310).

FREDERICK KIRCHHOFF

Indiana University–Purdue University at Fort Wayne

Chronology

1870   marriage. Publishes prose translation of *The Story of the Volsungs and Niblungs*.

1871   Leases Kelmscott Manor, Oxfordshire. Visits Iceland.

1872   Moves from Queen Square to Horrington House, Turnham Green. Publishes *Love is Enough*.

1873   Visits Northern Italy with Burne-Jones. Visits Iceland for the second time.

1875   The firm is dissolved and Morris becomes sole proprietor of Morris and Company. Publishes *Three Northern Love Stories* and a verse translation of the *Aeneid*.

1876   Publishes *The Story of Sigurd the Volsung and the Fall of the Niblungs*. Becomes treasurer of the Eastern Question Association.

1877   Founds the Society for the Protection of Ancient Buildings ("Anti-Scrape"). First public lectures. The firm opens a show room on Oxford Street.

1878   Moves to Kelmscott House, Hammersmith. Experiments with high-warp tapestry.

1881   Morris and Company moves its works to Merton Abbey, Surrey.

1883   Made honorary fellow of Exeter College, Oxford. Joins the Democratic Federation and declares himself a socialist. Reads Marx's *Das Kapital* in a French translation.

1884   Writes for the Social Democratic Federation journal *Justice*. Lectures for socialism on London street corners and in Scotland and the North of England. Resigns from the Federation.

1885   Joins in the formation of the Socialist League. Edits and backs the League's journal *Commonweal*. Arrested (and quickly discharged) at police court in connection with free speech demonstrations. Publishes *The Pilgrims of Hope*.

1886   Publishes *The Dream of John Ball* in *Commonweal*.

1887   Publishes translation of *The Odyssey*. "Bloody Sunday" (13 November Trafalgar Square demonstration broken up by police).

1888   Publishes collection of lectures, *Signs of Change*. Further lecturing on art and socialism. Completes first prose romance, *The House of the Wolfings*.

1889   Publishes *The Roots of the Mountains*. Attends International Conference of Socialists in Paris.

1890   Publishes *News from Nowhere* serially in *Commonweal*.

Leaves the Socialist League. Hammersmith branch renamed Hammersmith Socialist Society. Founds the Kelmscott Press.

1891 Publishes *The Story of the Glittering Plain*, *Poems by the Way*, and (with Magnússon) volume 1 of the *Saga Library*. In poor health.

1892 Sounded about Poet Laureateship at death of Tennyson (which he declines). Publishes volume 2 of *Saga Library*.

1893 With Belfort Bax, publishes *Socialism, Its Growth and Outcome* (previously serialized in *Commonweal*).

1894 Publishes *The Wood beyond the World*. Reconciled with the Social Democratic Federation.

1895 Translation of *The Tale of Beowulf*.

1896 Publishes *The Well at the World's End*. Kelmscott Press issues *The Works of Geoffrey Chaucer*. Visits Norway. Dies 3 October and is buried at Kelmscott 6 October.

1897 *The Water of the Wondrous Isles* and *The Sundering Flood* published posthumously.

1914 Death of Jane Morris.

CHAPTER 1

Life

I *Early Years (1834–1859)*

WILLIAM Morris was born on 24 March 1834, in Walthamstow, a village northeast of London. The family was well-to-do and, thanks to a lucky investment in copper mining, left rich at the death of Morris' father in 1847. Whatever Morris' later apologies for the "bourgeois style of comfort" and "rich establishmentarian puritanism"[1] of his childhood, Elm House and Woodford Hall, to which the family moved in 1840, provided a life-style he never ceased to cherish. Though it was near enough London for his father to commute daily to his office, Walthamstow was as yet isolated from the march of Victorian progress. "Woodford Hall brewed its own beer, and made its own butter, as much as a matter of course as it baked its own bread. Just as in the fourteenth century, there was a meal at high prime, midway between breakfast and dinner, when the children had cake and cheese and a glass of small ale."[2] Morris was even given a child's suit of armor, equipped in which he rode his pony through the paths of nearby Epping Forest.

An eldest son and, at first, a weak child, the boy had not only his mother but two older sisters to pamper him. Emma, four years his senior, appears to have played a particularly important role in Morris' emotional life.[3] He was not a spoiled child, but he seems to have had things much his own way, and the fits of rage he was given to as an adult suggest the indulgence of his early years.

Morris learned to read when he was very young, and by the time he was four had begun mastering Sir Walter Scott's Waverly novels. But he loved the outdoors too much to become bookish, and he showed only a desultory interest in formal education. In 1848 he entered the recently established Marlborough College, whose proximity to the Gothic and prehistoric monuments of Wilt-

shire and general high church flavor were more influential on
Morris than its disorganized academic curriculum. Christmas 1851,
after rioting against the headmaster—a taste of revolutionary uprising Morris was not to forget[4]—he left Marlborough; six months
later Morris passed the matriculation examination at Exeter College, Oxford, which he entered in the spring of 1853.

At Marlborough Morris was known as a solitary individual, who
took long walks by himself and invented stories "about knights and
fairies."[5] And it was not until he reached Oxford that Morris found
a set of companions to replace the close-knit family at Walthamstow. Here he met his lifelong friend Edward Burne-Jones (as
yet, plain "Jones") and fell in with the members of Burne-Jones'
Birmingham circle—Charles Faulkner, R. W. Dixon, William Ful-
ford, and, later, Cormell Price. Together, they read Tennyson,
Carlyle, and Ruskin, pored over medieval artifacts, and dreamed of
founding a monastic order—"the Brotherhood"—financed with the
nine hundred pounds a year income that came to Morris on his
twenty-first birthday. Morris never lost his aspirations for a communal society, but in time both he and Burne-Jones realized
that neither was cut out for the career in the church their families
expected of them. During a walking tour of northern France in the
summer of 1855, they recognized that it was art, not religion, that
attracted them to the Middle Ages; and as a consequence Burne-
Jones decided to become an artist, Morris an architect. Burne-
Jones left Oxford and began his new career under the tutelage of
Dante Gabriel Rossetti, the outspoken and controversial Pre-
Raphaelite painter and poet. Morris completed his final term in
the university and—much to the distress of his mother—articled
himself to G. E. Street, a Gothic-revivalist architect at that time
working in Oxford.

Morris had been writing verse for a good while, but it was not until
just after breakfast one morning in the spring of 1855 that he
presented Burne-Jones with what his friends believed his "first
poem." To Morris' Oxford circle, "The Willow and the Red Cliff"
"was a thing entirely new: founded on nothing previous: perfectly
original, whatever its value, and sounding truly striking and beautiful, extremely decisive and powerful in its execution. . . . He reached
his perfection at once." To which praise, Morris characteristically
replied, " 'Well, if this is poetry, it is very easy to write.' "[6] For a
while this "easy" poetry came thick and fast. Then, in the summer of

1855, the succession of verse gave way to the succession of short prose romances with which he diverted his friends for the next year.

No longer anticipating a quasi-monastic order under the patronage of Sir Galahad, the members of the brotherhood needed a new outlet for their creative energies. The result was *The Oxford and Cambridge Magazine*, published in twelve monthly numbers from January to December 1856. Morris financed the project and for a time acted as editor, but in the month of its first number he had already left the university and begun studying to be an architect. While he remained a regular contributor, *The Magazine* became largely a means for disposing of his literary work from the previous year, rather than a vehicle for current interests.

Morris threw himself with great energy into his work at Street's office—where he became fast friends with Philip Webb, the architect's senior clerk. At the same time, Burne-Jones had introduced him to Rossetti, through whom he became acquainted with other members of the Pre-Raphaelite Brotherhood. Late in the summer of 1856, Street transferred his office from Oxford to London, where Morris took rooms with Burne-Jones. Soon it became clear to Morris that painting, not architecture, was to be his life's work. For a while he divided his day between the two professions. But Rossetti's influence was too strong to resist, and by the end of 1856 he had left Street's office and moved, with Burne-Jones, to a set of rooms in Red Lion Square where there was space enough for both of them to work.

Thus began the bohemian period in Morris' life. His dress grew slovenly; his hair was allowed to grow thick and wild. And these superficial eccentricities signaled a profound break with the values of Walthamstow and Oxford. It was not the socialism of his later years that estranged Morris from his bourgeois antecedents, but his deliberate assumption of a profession and life-style his own family could only regard as a willful descent in society. Unlike Burne-Jones, whose admiration for Rossetti was tempered by a sense of his own mission as an artist, Morris exaggerated discipleship into obeisance—and thus laid the ground for his reaction against Rossetti in the late 1860s. But in 1857 Rossetti could do no wrong. The two young men entered wholeheartedly into Rossetti's project of decorating the library walls of the newly built Oxford Union Society with ten "frescoes" depicting scenes from Malory's *Morte Darthur*. With four other artists, they set to work without foresight or previous experience in painting on mortar. Morris was the first to begin and the first to finish. But his picture, "How Sir Palomydes loved La Belle Iseult with exceeding great love out of measure, and how she loved not him again but rather Sir Tristram"—as those of the other artists—had begun to fade before the end of the first year.

Despite the unhappy conclusion of the Union paintings, Morris continued to spend most of his time at Oxford. In addition to pursuing his work as a painter, he experimented with stone carving, embroidery, and the design of stained glass—and he also continued writing poetry. Rossetti admired Morris' poems, but had discouraged him from considering literature as a career. However, the poet Algernon Charles Swinburne, then a student at Oxford, was more enthusiastic. And during the last months of 1857 Morris wrote some of the best of his early poems. These, together with what he decided to rescue from his prior work, were published as *The Defence of Guenevere and Other Poems* in March of 1858. The volume, however, received little attention until after the success of *Jason* and *The Earthly Paradise* a decade later.

In 1857 at Oxford he had also become acquainted with Jane Burden, a striking and strangely beautiful young woman whom Rossetti had picked up at the theater and persuaded to sit for him as a model. Morris became engaged to her the following spring and on 26 April 1859, they were married. His marriage to the uneducated daughter of an Oxford stableman must have seemed a final humiliation to Morris' family, none of whom attended the wedding. Yet married life brought an end to the bohemianism of the 1850s. Moreover, it had become evident to Morris himself that painting, like architecture and the church, was turning into a dead end. When he returned to England after his six weeks honeymoon on the Continent, he was ready to begin a new phase in his life.

II   *Red House and the Early Years of the Firm (1859–1870)*

When Morris and Burne-Jones had moved into their rooms at Red Lion Square in 1856, Morris had been annoyed by the unavailability of plain, well-made commercial furniture and had paid a carpenter to build some pieces—a large round table, chairs, a settle, and a wardrobe—according to his own crude and rather heavy designs. Rossetti had then joined the two younger men in ornamenting this furniture with figures and inscriptions appropriate to its "intensely medieval"[7] appearance. Two years later, when Morris contemplated setting up a married household, he was once more faced with the same problem. This time, however, it was not just a matter of the right furniture, but also of the right house. And, as in the earlier instance, the only solution was to build them himself.

After considerable search, Morris chose a site for the house—an orchard near the small village of Upton in Kent, about ten miles southeast of London. Philip Webb, who had recently left Street's to open his own office, was the architect. But of course Morris himself took an active role, particularly in the interior design and furnishings. Webb's L-shaped plan and choice of material—the red brick from which "Red House" took its name—were highly original, as were the building's general severity of line and frank treatment of constructional elements. However, the project was to be more than the expression of one man and his architect. Underlying Morris' plan was the old urge toward communal life. His friends were drawn into the work of fabricating interior ornamentation and furnishings, and from the summer of 1860, when the Morrises moved into their new home, Red House was the center for regular weekend parties and longer visits by members of their circle. At one point, Morris almost succeeded in persuading Burne-Jones and his wife Georgiana (whom he had married in 1860) to consent for him to enlarge the house so that they could share it with him and Jane.

The five years Morris spent at Red House were the most satisfactory of his married life. Mistress of a substantial household, Jane found herself in a station she both understood and was gratified by. It was here, also, that Morris' two daughters, Jane ('Jenny') and Mary ('May'), were born. But activities set in motion by the construction of Red House were eventually instrumental in Morris' decision to move back to London. Mackail's description of the project suggests the effort entailed in setting up a home to Morris' specifications:

Not a chair, or table, or bed; not a cloth or paper hanging for the walls; nor tiles to line fireplaces or passages; nor a curtain or a candlestick; nor a jug to hold wine or a glass to drink out of, but had to be reinvented, one might almost say, to escape the flat ugliness of the current article. . . . Much of the furniture was specially designed by Webb and executed under his eye: the great oak dining-table, other tables, chairs, cupboards, massive copper candlesticks, fire-dogs, and table glass of extreme beauty.[8]

From the experience of "reinventing" these crafts for the benefit of one household, it was an easy step to a business devoted to

manufacturing the broad variety of articles necessary for a thorough-
going reform of British interior design. Thus, the firm of Morris,
Marshall, Faulkner and Company was founded.

The history of the firm is the history of Morris' development as a
designer, and as such exceeds the limits of this study. However, its
1861 prospectus suggests the range of the firm's initial activities.
Arguing that "the growth of Decorative Art in this country, owing to
the efforts of English Architects, has now reached a point at which it
seems desirable that artists of reputation should devote their time to
it," the members of the firm offer "to undertake any species of
decoration, mural or otherwise, from pictures, properly so called,
down to the consideration of the smallest work susceptible of art
beauty." Specifically,

They therefore now establish themselves as a firm for the production, by
themselves and under their supervision, of:
   I. Mural Decoration, either in Pictures or in Pattern Work, or merely
      in the arrangement of Colours, as applied to dwelling-houses,
      churches, or public buildings.
  II. Carving generally, as applied to Architecture.
 III. Stained Glass, especially with reference to its harmony with Mural
      Decoration.
  IV. Metal Work in all its branches, including Jewellery.
   V. Furniture, either depending for its beauty on its own design, on the
      application of materials hitherto overlooked, or on its conjunction
      with Figure and Pattern Painting. Under this head is included
      Embroidery of all kinds, Stamped Leather, and ornamental work in
      other such materials, besides every article necessary for domestic
      use. (II, ix–x)[9]

From the start, ecclesiastical institutions were among the firm's
major customers, stained glass its most successful work. In time,
however, Morris and Company gradually shifted its emphasis from
individually designed articles to the carefully controlled mass production of wallpapers, fabrics, and carpets.

As business developed, it became clear that Morris himself, who
had soon assumed the role of leading member, would have to live
closer to the place of manufacture. There was talk of moving the
workshop to Upton, but instead, in 1865, Morris moved both family
and firm to Queen Square, Bloomsbury. In part, the unhealthy
location and chilly design of Red House had dictated this decision;
nevertheless, the move from her grand home in the country to rooms
over a workshop appears to have marked the beginning of Jane's

estrangement from her husband, which in turn led to her growing involvement with Rossetti, whose public attentions became the subject of gossip. Meanwhile, as Morris' copper shares had begun to pay lower and lower dividends, he turned increasingly to the firm as a source of income—at a time when, undercapitalized and poorly managed, it was itself in danger of bankruptcy.

Morris' plan to compose a series of verse narratives has a long history, but it was not until the move to Queen Square that he began to work in earnest on *The Earthly Paradise*. It was hard for Morris to conceive of himself as a businessman rather than an artist with an independent income, and he had a difficult time controlling his habitually lavish expenditures. Thus, in addition to providing him with a respite from the double strain of his souring marriage and precarious finances, his return to writing poetry reflects a genuine crisis in identity. At first simply a means of escape—particularly in Morris' original conception of a "decorated book" with copious illustrations by Burne-Jones[10]—*The Earthly Paradise* evolved into complex, morally significant poetry.

Morris was further prompted to complete the massive collection of stories—it came to surpass 42,000 lines of verse—by the unexpected success of his *Life and Death of Jason* in 1867. *Jason* had been planned as one of the *Earthly Paradise* tales, but grew so long that it had to come out as a separate piece. For Morris, whose only prior volume of poetry had been a financial and critical failure, the immediate popularity of his first extended narrative poem was a happy event. *Jason* went into a second printing within the year and encouraged Morris to work steadily on the twenty-four poems he intended for *The Earthly Paradise*, which itself outgrew his plan for a work in one volume. The first twelve stories (parts 1 and 2) were published separately in 1868, while both part 3, which came out in December 1869, and part 4, which appeared a year later, required individual volumes. To some extent the changes in his original conception of the work—which involve substituting new stories as well as increasing the overall length—derive from the sheer pleasure Morris found in composing the poems. But they are also a result of the self-knowledge he gained by writing *The Earthly Paradise* itself.

III *Kelmscott and Iceland (1871–1880)*

In 1871 Morris joined Rossetti in leasing Kelmscott Manor as a secondary residence and took the first of his two journeys to Iceland.

Both gestures were turning points in his life; both places became central images in his work. "A heaven on earth," he described the house to Faulkner. Situated in an "out of the way corner" of Oxfordshire where "people built Gothic till the beginning or middle of the last century," Kelmscott Manor embodied the architectural continuity with the medieval past Morris so highly prized. He found it "a beautiful and strangely naif house," with "a sadness about it, which is not gloom but the melancholy born of beauty . . . very stimulating to the imagination" (*Letters*, 41–46).

Morris' attitude toward his marriage and the relationship between Jane and Rossetti during this period is difficult to fix. Jane, whose intellectual limitations had always stood in the way of a complete understanding between husband and wife, became increasingly uninterested in Morris' work and aspirations; her manner, increasingly aloof, silent, and hypochondriacal. Morris seems to have interpreted this as a personal failure to realize his own romantic ideal, rather than the joint failure of two individuals to sustain a union. Thus he was alternately disturbed and relieved by Jane's attachment to someone who could free him from his sense of responsibility to her. The extent of the intimacy between Jane and Rossetti remains a matter of conjecture. Victorians were generally reticent about such matters, and Rossetti's relationships with women were often obsessions with the symbolic roles in which he cast them, rather than straightforward sexual liasons. He used her as a model for his paintings; he sat at her feet and fed her strawberries; he flattered her beauty—at a time when she must have begun to think of herself as no longer young; he pampered her "illnesses"—when Morris was more concerned with seeing her in good health. He had both the time and the inclination to give her the attentions she no longer as amply received from her husband. And Morris, who had strong feelings about the importance of sexual freedom, did not stand in the way of their being with each other as often as they wished. Indeed, leasing Kelmscott Manor jointly with Rossetti seems to have been prompted by Morris' desire to provide the couple with a place in which they could live together respectably. This, however, did not prevent Rossetti himself from becoming more and more a source of annoyance, whom Morris avoided whenever he could. Hence, with Rossetti in copossession, Kelmscott Manor could not yet become fully Morris' own. "Not only does he keep me from that harbour of refuge," he complained to Aglaia Coronio in November 1872, "(because it is really a farce our meeting when we can help it) but also he has all sorts of ways so unsympathetic with the sweet simple old place, that I feel his presence there as a kind of slur on it" (*Letters*, 51).

In antithesis to the gentle scale of the Oxfordshire landscape, Iceland provided an example of stoic endurance in the face of poverty and hardship Morris was never to forget. The sheer physical exertion of his two journeys (with Eiríkr Magnússon, Charles Faulkner, and W. H. Evans in 1871 and with Faulkner and two Icelandic guides in 1873) played an important role in shaking him out of the passive despondency of the *Earthly Paradise* years. "Surely I have gained a great deal and it was no idle whim that drew me there, but a true instinct for what I needed" (*Letters*, 59), he explained on his return in 1873. (In contrast, his trip to Florence and Sienna with Burne-Jones in the spring of the same year was less than a success, and Morris annoyed his companion by "merchandizing for the Firm" [*Letters*, 56] rather than devoting himself to art.)

Iceland and its poetry had a profound influence on Morris' literary career. And the extensive journals he kept throughout the first and during the earlier stages of the second expedition dramatize the significance of the experience in reshaping his general outlook on life. It would be misleading to reduce the influence of Iceland on Morris to a simple cause-and-effect relationship. However, the year after the second journey marked a decisive change in his personal affairs. By threatening to give up his share of the lease, he forced Rossetti to relinquish half interest in Kelmscott Manor; and he effected a reorganization of the firm through which it was brought under his sole control. (In 1867, the firm had been commissioned to decorate the Green Dining Room at St. James's Palace, and during the last years of the decade its products were beginning to find a market in the fashionable element of the middle class. But profits came slowly, and it was not until the 1870 death of Warrington Taylor, the firm's business manager, that Morris seems to have fully grasped the need to live within his narrowed income, and not until the mid 1870s that he finally accepted the role of artisan-businessman and could enter into the work of Morris and Company with total commitment.)

The 1870s also marked the commencement of Morris' social activism. Despite the horror of many Englishmen over Turkish atrocities in the Balkans, the prime minister refused to side with Russia, on the verge of war with Turkey, and maintained instead a position favorable to the Turks. For Morris, it appeared that the British government was about to use its military and naval power in defense of Turkish despotism. Consequently, in October 1876, he addressed a letter "England and the Turks" to the editor of *The Daily News*, in which he castigated Disraeli's imperialist "war on behalf of the thieves and murderers!" "I who am writing this," Morris felt the need to explain, "am one of a large class of men—quiet men, who usually go about their own business, heeding public matters less than they ought, and afraid to speak in such a huge concourse as the English nation, however much they may feel, but who are now stung into bitterness by thinking how helpless they are in a public matter that touches them so closely" (*Letters*, 82). Elected treasurer of the Eastern Question Association (an organization aimed at influencing British foreign policy against the Turks), Morris had his first taste of organized protest—and the Association's failure to enlist the support of the Liberal Party when the tide of public opinion shifted in favor of the Turks in 1878 was the first stage in his political radicalization. Less than a year later than the October 1876 letter, another letter to the editor—in this instance, objecting to the "destruction" of Tewkesbury Minster under the guise of "restoration" (*Letters*, 85–86)—led to founding the Society for the Protection of Ancient Buildings (fondly termed "Anti-Scrape"). Also in 1877, Morris gave the first of his many lectures, "The Decorative Arts." He was fast becoming a public figure. The next year, after a journey to Italy with his family—marred by an attack of gout—Morris moved into Kelmscott House, Hammersmith, which remained his London residence until the end of his life.

The literary history of this period in Morris' development begins with his introduction to the "real Icelander" Eiríkr Magnússon in 1868. Magnússon agreed to teach Morris Icelandic, and together they undertook a series of translations from the sagas: *The Story of Gunnlaug the Wormtongue* (1869), *The Story of Grettir the Strong* (1869), *The Story of the Volsungs and the Fall of the Niblungs* (1870), together with a group of shorter tales published in the collection *Three Northern Love Stories* (1875). Morris' two verse adaptations of Icelandic saga in *The Earthly Paradise*—"The Lovers of Gudrun" and "The Fostering of Aslaug"—also date from this period. In his original writing, *Love is Enough* (1872) marks the transition between the aesthetic of *The Earthly Paradise* and that of the North. And six years after his prose translation of the Volsunga Saga, Morris completed its verse adaptation, *The Story of Sigurd the Volsung and the Fall of the Niblungs* (1876), the work that he regarded as the masterpiece of his career as a poet.

IV *The Decade of Activism (1881–1890)*

In 1881 Morris moved the firm's manufacturing works from Queen Square to Merton Abbey, in the suburbs south of London. Here, on the banks of the River Wandle—which furnished the pure water necessary for dyeing—amid poplar and willow trees and an old-fashioned flower garden, Morris was able to approximate the working conditions of his ideal factory: "a group of people working in harmonious co-operation towards a useful end" in a setting "pleasant as to its surroundings, and beautiful in its architecture," where "even the rough and necessary work . . . might be so arranged as to be neither burdensome in itself or of long duration for each worker"[11]. This precise formulation came later; the ideal itself predates Morris' philosophical commitment to socialism. His confidence in the creative potential of ordinary human beings derived from his habit of assigning the first available man to whatever new skill the work of the firm made necessary. Moreover, his workmen produced nothing the actual fabrication of which Morris himself had not mastered. Ruskin had taught him the fatality of separating the intellectual task of design from the physical labor of manufacture. But in his own case, the pleasure of manual work was sufficient incentive for its mastery. And what he knew he himself could do, Morris took it for granted most other men under the right conditions could accomplish. "My work is little else than pleasure to me," he explained in a letter to *The Manchester Examiner.* "Under no conceivable circumstances would I give it up even if I could. Over and over again have I asked myself why should not my lot be the common lot. My work is simple work enough; much of it, nor that the least pleasant, any man of decent intelligence could do, if he could but get to care about the work and its results" (*Letters,* 166). He paid his employees well, and whenever possible "he substituted piece work founded on the advanced rates of wages for the time work . . . thus giving the workman a greater liberty as to disposal of his time. . . . Piece workers . . . could then occasionally knock off for an hour's work in the garden—the garden having been allotted in sections to the piece workers."[12] That workers should share in the profits of the firm seemed only natural to a capitalist who thought of himself as a worker. His employees were an enlarged family, in which the authority of the employer derived from his example of hard work and initiative rather than from his ability to reward or punish. "To my mind," he wrote in 1883, "no man is good enough to be any one's master without injuring himself, at least, whatever he does for the servant" (*Letters*, 177). No theoretical proposition, his view simply reflects the relationship with his workmen in which Morris felt most comfortable.

Morris had converted the coach house and stables at Kelmscott House into a weaving room and installed the looms on which the first "Hammersmith" carpets were produced by the firm. The facilities at Merton enabled him to design and supervise the execution of much larger carpets. Similarly, when he had moved into Kelmscott House Morris had had a tapestry loom built in his bedroom, at which he practiced weaving, often for several hours early in the morning. At Merton these experiments led to his reviving the manufacture of high-warp arras tapestry. The production of chintzes, which Morris had carried on—not entirely to his satisfaction—through a subsidiary, was also transferred to Merton. These cotton textiles became the most broadly popular of the firm's manufactures.

With the exception of a few items, like the rush-bottomed Sussex chairs popularized by the firm, Morris and Company's products were generally priced beyond the means of any but the upper middle and upper classes. As the firm became more fashionable, Morris found himself increasingly the purveyor of goods and services to the classes of British society he held in greatest contempt. In setting standards of beauty and integrity of household goods, Morris and Company was a success; in extending them to the common man, it was a failure. Thus, the firm at once gave Morris firsthand experience of a mode of production more humane and, in the quality of its workmanship, more satisfactory than the factory system and intensified his alienation from the ruling class of Victorian England.

E. P. Thompson argues that Morris' experience in the "Anti-Scrape" movement—in which he continued to play an active role—strongly influenced his conversion to socialism. The dogged unwillingness of men in positions of power to comprehend the value of Britain's architectural heritage faced him again and again with the spiritual poverty of bourgeois culture. Reform—the work of his own firm—was inadequate; only a full-scale revolution would bring about the social conditions necessary for the genuine love of beauty. The actual stages in his "conversion" may never be fully explicated. It involved a period of dalliance with Ruskinian socialism in the late 1870s, during which he delivered lectures to what was intended to be a workingmen's association (the "Trades Guild of Learning") and a short-lived infatuation with Gladstone's Liberal platform. But Gladstone's performance as prime minister was profundly disappointing—particularly, for Morris, his capitulation to the jingoism he had opposed in his 1880 campaign. The Eastern Question Association was Morris' first connection with radical members of the working class. Subsequently, in 1879, as treasurer of the National Liberal League, he associated himself—to little avail—with Labor support of Gladstone. What he learned from both experiences was not the political potential of the working class, but its vulnerability within a political system dominated by the middle class.

Though long familiar with the socioeconomic writings of Ruskin, Morris was "blankly ignorant of economics" and of Marxist thought in general (XXIII, 277) until 1882, when he began reading socialist literature and attended a series of public lectures on the principles of socialism. In January 1883, eager "to join any body who distinctly called themselves socialists" (*Letters*, 188), he became a member of H. M. Hyndman's Democratic Federation, and the next month began the laborious task of reading a French translation of Marx's *Kapital*. Finally, in November of that year, he concluded a lecture on "Art under Plutocracy" at University College, Oxford, with a public declaration of his conversion to socialism and an appeal to his audience to "unite with those whose aims are right, and their means honest and feasible" (XXIII, 191).

Morris soon found himself an important member of the Democratic Federation. His conversion to the movement had bewildered and estranged many of his oldest friends, and to some of the socialists his credentials were suspect. (Engels persisted in calling him a "poet"; Morris himself preferred to be known as a "Designer.") Nevertheless he was quickly accepted as a leader. Elected to the Federation's executive, he lectured in England and Scotland and spoke at open-air meetings on behalf of its program. He wrote for its journal, *Justice*—and sold it on street corners. The year after he joined, the Federation changed its náme to the Social-Democratic Federation and, to Morris' pleasure, adopted an explicitly socialist platform: "The Socialization of the Means of Production, Distribution and Exchange to be controlled by a Democratic State in the interests of the entire community, and the complete Emancipation of Labour from the domination of Capitalism and Landlordism, with the Establishment of Social and Economic Equality between the Sexes."[13] However, dissention within the executive, largely owing to Hyndman's proprietary view of the organization, led to a split in its ranks. A majority of the executive, including Morris, Edward Aveling, Eleanor Marx, and Belfort Bax, withdrew from the Social-Democratic Federation and in December 1884 founded the Socialist League.

During his two years in the Federation, Morris had become one of the central figures in British socialism. Now, as treasurer of the Socialist League and editor of its organ (*Commonweal*)—jointly with Aveling at first, later with Bax—Morris was the leading figure in what came close to being his own organization. He traveled indefatigably, addressing public gatherings and branches of the League. He took an active role in the struggle to affirm the socialists' right to free speech in public, which was being opposed by concerted police harassment, on two occasions found himself before a magistrate, and consciously risked imprisonment. Under his editorship *Commonweal* became a significant organ of Marxist thought. Engels himself was an early contributor, and Morris wrote some of his most important socialist essays for the journal. In addition, the monthly (later weekly) issues of *Commonweal* contained Morris' extended narrative poem on the Paris Commune, *The Pilgrims of Hope* (1885); a series of articles he coauthored with Bax, *Socialism from the Root Up* (1886–1887), republished in 1893 as *Socialism: Its Growth and Outcome;* and his two socialist romances, *A Dream of John Ball* (1886–1887) and *News from Nowhere* (1890).

The weakness of the Socialist League lay in its inability to recognize that a genuine socialist movement could not be imposed on the workers by middle-class theoreticians. This inability lay behind the League's refusal to participate in the formation of a labor party at a time when immediate political gains seemed most attractive to the working class. Despite his intellectual acknowledgment that the future of British socialism lay with the workers, Morris was never able to bridge the gap between his class and theirs. During the 1880s he was committed to the belief that any measures to ameliorate the conditions of the poor short of revolution were counterrevolutionary in nature. As more and more socialists rejected this ideological purism, Morris found himself isolated in the extreme left of the movement, with the result that the Socialist League was ultimately taken over by its anarchist element.

The single most formative experience of this period was the Trafalgar Square Riot of 1887 ("Bloody Sunday"). In protest against a police ban on demonstrations by the London unemployed, a large body of socialists and other radicals attempted a free-speech rally in

Trafalgar Square and were attacked with gunfire by a force of policemen and soldiers. Morris' presence at a genuine physical confrontation between social classes—hundreds were wounded and three men killed—confirmed his belief that revolution would entail bloodshed. However, the ease with which the London police brutally dispersed a large but undisciplined gathering of protestors dispelled Morris' confidence in a socialist revolution at any time in the near future and ultimately led to his withdrawal from fully active participation in the movement.

V *Last Years (1891–1896)*

In May 1890 Morris was ejected from the editorship of *Commonweal*, which was now in the hands of the anarchists. In November of that year the Hammersmith branch seceded from the Socialist League and took the name Hammersmith Socialist Society. From this point in his life, Morris moved away from the forefront of British socialism. As a leader he had failed on several counts. His original decision to leave the Social-Democratic Federation had created a split in the movement that seriously weakened its credibility with the workers it sought to enlist. He had permitted the Socialist League to depend too much on his (substantial) financial support and personal magnetism. And his ideological "purism" had allowed the League to fall into the hands of an extremist minority. However, Morris did not turn his back on socialism after 1890. He simply withdrew from day-to-day political affairs. He was pleased to see the various socialist parties resolving their differences, and in 1894 he finally reconciled himself with the Social-Democratic Federation. No longer the leader of a faction, Morris at last assumed his place as spokesman for the movement as a whole. He continued to preside at meetings of the Hammersmith Socialist Society, but these increasingly took on the character of Sunday evenings-at-home, with Morris the center of a gathering of admirers—or curiosity seekers. He continued to write socialist essays, no longer for a single periodical, but for journals representing a divergent range of opinion. And still with some regularity he continued to speak on behalf of "the Cause."

Other interests continued as well. He continued to spend as much time as he could spare at Kelmscott Manor, the lease for which he renewed for a twenty-year term. The work of the firm went on. His commitment to the Society for the Protection of Ancient Buildings was unabated—and now broadened to a general interest in conservation. However, the two great achievements of his last six years—the prose romances and, to a greater extent, the work of the Kelmscott Press—necessarily drew him from these earlier concerns.

Morris' interest in fine printing was not altogether new.[14] His attempt to publish *The Earthly Paradise* with illustrations by Burne-Jones had failed, largely because of the incongruous relationship between the engravings, over which he had optimum control, and the letterpress, over which he had little if any. With the exception of designing the first edition of *Love is Enough*, Morris appears to have renounced hope in nineteenth-century printing, until the reawakening of his interest in the late 1880s. For many years he had admired illuminated manuscripts and early printed books and from time to time had purchased such of both as had caught his fancy. Now he devoted time and money to amassing a collection of the best examples of medieval printing and calligraphy to use as a standard against which to measure his own work.

Typically, once Morris had determined to rediscover yet another lost art, he realized he would not be satisfied until he had the entire process of book design and manufacture under his own supervision. In January 1891 he rented a cottage near Kelmscott House and set up a printing press. The first book produced by the Kelmscott Press was his romance, *The Story of the Glittering Plain*, which appeared that spring. Then came a collection of his miscellaneous poetry, *Poems by the Way* (1891). The press subsequently published fifty-one more titles, totaling over 18,000 volumes. In addition to his own works, these included editions of the nineteenth-century poets whom Morris admired—Coleridge, Keats, Shelley, Tennyson, Rossetti, and Swinburne—and, as one might expect, of the medieval writers who had meant most to him throughout his life. The output of the press was thus a gesture of honoring—and commemorating—the men whose achievement had influenced his own, and as such was as strong an act of self-definition as any in Morris' development. Equally important, Kelmscott Press editions were designed to be read slowly and thus constitute a statement about the proper relationship between a book and its reader. In an era in which the growth of the publishing industry had begun to produce the "plague of books" we increasingly suffer in the twentieth century, Morris asked us to treat his favorite works as treasures to be savored—rather than courses for speed-reading. Morris himself designed the typefaces and took pains to secure the finest materials with which to work. Although a few were cheap, most of the productions of the Kelmscott Press were expensive—and have continued to increase in value to the present day. They were, in other words, unabashedly luxury items. Freed of his former compunctions about producing goods for the upper class, Morris had finally given in to the sheer pleasure of fine craftsmanship.

Written in the spring of 1890, *The Story of the Glittering Plain* was the first of the prose romances Morris composed in accelerating succession, initially as a respite from his other activities, later as a central preoccupation. It was followed by *The Wood Beyond the World* (1894), *Child Christopher and Goldilind the Fair* (1895), *The Well at the World's End* (1896), and the posthumously published *Water of the Wondrous Isles* (1897) and *Sundering Flood* (1897). Related in genre to his earliest writings for *The Oxford and Cambridge Magazine* and, of course, to the socialist romances of the 1880s, they also connect Morris with the exploration of myth and symbolism carried out in the first decades of the twentieth century by writers like Yeats, Joyce, and Eliot. This concern, together with their profound psychological awareness, argues that the romances were by no means the regression they were judged by some of Morris' contemporaries. (Shaw called them "a startling relapse into literary pre-Raphaelitism," *MM*, II, xxviii.) On the contrary, they are a natural and wholly satisfactory summation of Morris' career as a writer.

However the prose romances were not his sole literary work during the 1890s. Returning to collaboration with Magnusson, he began publishing a series of translations from the Icelandic under the general title *The Saga Library*. And in 1895 the Kelmscott Press published what is perhaps his most remarkable translation, *The Tale of Beowulf*. Again, we find Morris finally bringing himself to do the things he had always wanted to do.

Morris never fully recovered health after a severe attack of gout and kidney infection in 1891. From this time on in his life, he spoke of himself as an "invalid." It is customary for biographers to observe that the years of unrelenting activity had taken their toll on his system. It would be more accurate to say that Morris had simply begun to conceive of himself as an old man. In the summer of 1896 he took his last journey to the North—a voyage along the coast of Norway. Fittingly, a month before he left, the Kelmscott Press issued its most important achievement, *The Works of Geoffrey Chaucer* (the so-called "Kelmscott Chaucer"). He returned from Norway "somewhat

better, but hated the voyage" and "so glad to be home" (*Letters*, 385).
A few weeks later he was stricken with congestion of the left lung. His
condition steadily deteriorated, and on 3 October 1896 he died
quietly in his bed at Kelmscott House. Three days later, Morris was
buried in Kelmscott churchyard.

CHAPTER 2

"A Thing Entirely New": Morris' Early Poetry and Prose

AMONG his friends, Morris' first serious efforts as a writer caused a sensation. That he revealed himself as a poet was in itself a surprise. (He had not until then *seemed* in the least like a poet.) But, more remarkably, what he wrote was informed with a spontaneity and daring his university circle—although initially few others—unhesitatingly prized. It is possible to detect the influences of Browning, Rossetti, Ruskin, Poe, and even Tennyson in Morris' early poetry and prose. Yet its originality stamps it as the firstfruits of a significant creative mind.

I *The* Oxford and Cambridge Magazine *Romances (1856)*

Morris published five poems in *The Oxford and Cambridge Magazine;* however, most of his contributions were prose: eight romances, a review of Browning's *Men and Women,* and descriptive articles on Amiens Cathedral and two engravings by Alfred Rethel.

The Browning review is a prime document in Morris' development as a poet, and his remarks on two poems are particularly significant—"Cleon," with which he opens the essay, and "Childe Roland to the Dark Tower Came," which he "loves best." The multifaceted pagan artist, acutely conscious of the limits to creativity in "these latter days," Browning's Cleon has much in common with Morris himself, and his frustrated desire for intensity of life elicits Morris' strongest sympathy. On the other hand, Cleon's elitism—inescapably similar to the elitism of the brotherhood—frightens Morris into a denunciation of revealing passion: "he would bring about, if he could, a most dreary aristocracy of intellect, where the commoners would be bound hand and foot, mere slaves to the great men and their great lordly minds, not loyal freemen, honouring the heroes" (I, 326).

If Cleon typifies the alienated aesthete Morris fears he may become, Childe Roland represents the heroic figure he wishes to be. But this identification is only possible because his interpretation of "Childe Roland" is a radical misreading of the poem. "It may in some sort be an allegory," he explains. "But that is not its first meaning; neither, as some poeple think, was it written for the sake of the fearful pictures . . . for the poet's real design was to show us a brave man doing his duty, making his way on to his point through all dreadful things. What do all these horrors matter to him? He must go on, they cannot stop him; he will be slain certainly, who knows by what unheard-of death; yet he can leave all this in God's hands, and go forward, for it will all come right at the end" (I, 339). Nothing in Browning's poem indicates that his protagonist is "a brave man," much less that he is "doing his duty," "will be slain certainly," or is "in God's hands." Moreover, Morris' assumption that "it will all come right at the end" triumphantly ignores the inconclusiveness central to the meaning of the poem.[1]

But the ambiguities Morris evades in his interpretation of Childe Roland's quest were not easily laid to rest. The heroes of his own romances are denied the privilege of passing "straight from our eyes to the place where the true and brave live for ever"; and, much as Morris may have wished to portray "brave men doing their duty," it is the allegory and "fearful pictures" of his romances that bear the weight of their significance.

Just where the narrator of "The Story of the Unknown Church" has passed is not at all clear. "I was the master-mason of a church that was built more than six hundred years ago," he tells us in the opening of the tale. "I do not remember very much about the land where my church was; I have quite forgotten the name of it, but I know it was very beautiful, and even now, while I am thinking of it, comes a flood of old memories" (I, 149). The deictic "now" is coyly misleading, the locus of the narrator deliberately unexplained. However, these ambiguities are essential to Morris' intentions, as becomes clear when we place "The Story of the Unknown Church" in context with the essay on Amiens Cathedral Morris was writing at the same time. The essay is modeled on Ruskin's *Stones of Venice* (a work he greatly admired). But Morris carries Ruskin's empathetic re-creation of medieval society to a curious extreme. In order to reconstruct the past, he places himself in personal relationship with a set of fictitious men and women: "thinking of their passed-away builders I can see through them very faintly, dimly, some little of the mediaeval times, else dead and gone from me for ever; voiceless for ever. And those same builders, still surely living, still real men and capable of receiving love, I love no less than the great men, poets and painters and such like, who are on earth now; no less than my breathing friends whom I can see looking kindly on me now" (I, 349). Morris' need to "love" the constructs of his own fantasy suggests something incomplete or inadequate in his relationship with his "breathing friends." Indeed, his claim that he "can see" those friends "looking kindly on me now" transforms them, too, into fantasy. If his early writing was at once a means of creating a set of (imaginary) supportive figures and winning the approval of a set of (real) friends that his imagination tended to perceive through the structures of literary fantasy (i.e., in terms of "the Brotherhood"), then these purposes were at odds with his writing a simple, factual description of Amiens Cathedral. He had trouble completing the article and abandoned his plan to write on other French churches.

What he wrote instead was "The Story of the Unknown Church," the narrator of which is one of those "passed-away builders . . . still surely living" he evokes in the Amiens essay. The story has a rudimentary plot: the master mason Walter, at work with his sister Margaret on the final carvings of the nearly completed church, falls into a sequence of dreams involving the figure of Amyot, his own closest friend and his sister's betrothed, who left five years earlier to fight "in the holy wars." He rouses from his fantasies to see Amyot before him. The next morning he finds Amyot dead. Margaret says farewell and she, too, dies, but Walter lives on "very lonely and sad." Thinking to die himself when it is complete, he begins carving their tomb in the church. But the task lengthens; he enters the monastery to which the church is attached; finally, after twenty years' labor, "they found me lying dead, with my chisel in my hand, underneath the last lily of the tomb" (I, 158).

The story's derivation from the article on Amiens Cathedral explains the indeterminate locus of its narrative voice—Walter is primarily a relationship with the past, not a character in a work of fiction—but it does not explain why Walter's life presents such a negative view of the Middle Ages. Sexually unfulfilled, his life dwindles into a solipsistic celebration of death—his life's work, a monument soon forgotten in time. And what remains is a collage of brilliant natural images: "glimpses of the great golden corn sea, waving, waving, waving for leagues and leagues; and among the corn grew burning scarlet poppies, and blue corn-flowers; and the corn-flowers were so blue, that they gleamed, and seemed to burn with a steady light, as they grew beside the poppies among the gold of the wheat" (I, 150). The reiterated "burn" is characteristic of the narrator's vision. He recollects a natural world whose very intensity approaches self-destruction. The church is gone, but "if you knew the place, you would see the heaps made by the earth-covered ruins heaving with the yellow corn into glorious waves, so that the place where my church used to be is as beautiful now as when it stood in all its splendour" (I, 149).

Thus, a story intended as an evocation of the spirit of medieval architecture transforms itself into a celebration of the futility of art. Nowhere else is Morris' ambivalence toward human achievement more inescapable than in his ecstatic description of nature reassuming sway over the ruins of Walter's church. And when we recollect that Morris himself began studying architecture the same month the story was printed, it is difficult not to perceive the story as an expression of misgivings about his own creative potential.

A voice from limbo, the master mason of the Unknown Church is a far cry from Childe Roland faring "straight from our eyes to the place where the true and brave live for ever." But the first-person narrator of "The Hollow Land" is an even more ambiguous hero. Florian's story is among the most elusively symbolic in Morris' work. It begins with his brother Arnald's insult at the hands of Swanhilda and his Christmas Eve revenge, years later, when she is put brutally to death. Defying retaliation, the House of the Lilies gathers to defend itself, but—in an unconscious admission of guilt—leaves the city and regresses to a nomadic life in the hills. Reduced to cattle stealing, the House is attacked by Swanhilda's son Red Harald and once more stricken with an uncanny loss of courage. Left fighting alone, Arnald and then Florian plunge over a cliff into "the Hollow Land." At the opening of the final chapter, Florian awakens in a pastoral landscape where he meets his love Margaret. They live together idyllically, until they come upon a woman in scarlet, sobbing, whose presence in the Hollow Land Margaret cannot explain. The story breaks without transition, and Florian reawakens "on a horrible grey November day" in the same spot to which he first fell. But he has aged, and his helmet has rusted and is filled with "a lump of slimy earth with worms coiled up in it." Plunging into a stream, he is rescued by a man in scarlet raiment "with upright stripes of yellow and black all over it," who spears his shoulder with a barbed fish-spear. Again he passes into dream, then reawakens naked before his family castle, now fallen into

ruin. Once more he encounters the man in scarlet, who is painting
figures of Harald, Arnald, Swanhilda, Florian, and a beautiful woman
Florian cannot identify (presumably Margaret) as "God's judg-
ments" on the interior walls. They fight; the stranger is wounded;
Florian nurses him back to health; he teaches Florian to paint and
together they continue the sequence of red and yellow frescoes. After
many years, the cortege of a dead king passes. Without explanation,
Florian calls, "O Harald, let us go!" and they set forth for the Hollow
Land. The woman in scarlet reappears, and Harald elects to stay
behind with her, but Florian regains Margaret and they enter into "a
hollow city in the Hollow Land."

"The Hollow Land" is Morris' revision of "Childe Roland." The
misdeeds of Roland's peers become Arnald's needless revenge on the
self-tortured Swanhilda and the general degeneration of the House of
the Lilies. The subjective landscape of Roland's quest corresponds to
the surreal landscape of the second chapter of the romance. But the
third part, which supplies the conclusion missing in Browning's
poem, entails a striking reversal of Morris' interpretation of "Childe
Roland." His first encounter with the Hollow Land gives Florian the
awareness of a life his brutal version of the chivalric code has
precluded. But the function of the earthly paradise is to give shape to
the process of renewal through art he undergoes with Red Harald in
"Hell." Converting his experience into aesthetic form prepares him
for the higher version of the Hollow Land he discovers in the final
episode of the romance. Reaching the gateway to the heavenly city,
Margaret and Florian see their own "winged and garlanded" figures
carved on the arch. They enter because they have become facets of
the architecture. And yet there is no one inside—only "a great space
of flowers." Morris needs the archetype of the heavenly city to
complete Florian's quest, but he cannot bring himself to fill it with
heavenly beings. As in "The Story of the Unknown Church," human
achievement gives way to the beauty of the natural world. Thus
Florian neither "passes straight" nor into "the place where the true
and the brave live for ever." And what emerges from the allegory and
"fearful pictures" of his quest is the implication that the artist's work is
a purgation of sin, for which he gains at best an uncertain reward.

A similar concern with guilt informs "Lindenborg Pool." Based on
material he had been reading in Benjamin Thorpe's *Northern
Mythology*, the story—by Morris' account (I, 245)—rose spontane-
ously into his conscious mind. Its narrator is a man of the nineteenth
century who obsessively returns to the place where he killed an

unspecified adversary—"not undeservedly, God knows, yet how dreadful it was!" Amid the tumult of a stormy night, he attempts to fathom the hitherto unfathomed pool and in the process falls into yet another of the dreams that characterize these early tales. He is at once himself and a medieval priest called to administer the last sacrament to a "bad bold Lord," only to become the butt of a macabre practical joke. In the midst of androgynous, hallucinatory reveling, he is tricked into giving the host to a swine, who rolls out of the bedclothes and scores his hand with its tusk. Seizing a sword, the wounded priest cuts his way through the melee and escapes the castle, which then collapses in a cloud of dust and sinks—like Poe's House of Usher— into the newly created pool.

Attempting to find a bottom to this "dreadful pool" is clearly a gesture of self-investigation, and the narrator's double consciousness in the dream—thirteenth-century priest and gentleman "in service-able broadcloth of the nineteenth century"—objectifies Morris' sense of inner division. What is remarkable is his negative treatment of both characters. The modern gentleman is a murderer and the priest a dupe. Seen as a reflection of Morris' decision to renounce a career in the church, the story suggests his fear that attempting to realize a medieval ideal of priesthood would make him the mocked and symbolically emasculated figure of the story. Taking up a sword, the priest rejects his passive role and so doing both reasserts his masculine identity and clarifies the ambiguous guilt of the narrator. Becoming—against his will—a man of violence, the priest slays his former, socially imposed identity, just as Morris had broken with "society" by rejecting his family's ambitions for his future.

Normally the traumatic rejection of family values occurs during adolescence. For Morris, it came at a time when the need to make serious decisions about his career made his position all the more difficult. But the priest role stands for a constellation of values of which the approval of Walthamstow is only one. Throughout his life Morris felt a strong need for communal support—whether from family, friends, business associates, or political allies. At the same time, he was also a strongly individualistic, strongly aggressive personality. Giving way to the aggressive element—as he did at the end of his years at Oxford—precipitated feelings of anxiety, to some extent temporary, to some extent typical of those he would continue to face.

The other stories he published in *The Oxford and Cambridge*

Magazine lead to similar insights into Morris' psychology. The longest, "Gertha's Lovers," centers on a love triangle foreshadowing the relationship that was to develop between Morris, Jane, and Rossetti. We see still another example of Morris' fascination with heroic failure in his portrayal of Leuchnar—the "sallow," "troubled," and misunderstood outsider who proves his manhood fighting on behalf of the woman whose love will always belong to the heroic, blond Olaf, his king and friend. In "Svend and His Brethren," on the other hand, Siur is really loved, but renounced by Cissela in order that she may save her people by marrying the tyrant who threatens their freedom. Siur follows her to the enemy capital, where as court armorer he eventually enables her children (Svend and his brethren) to save themselves by fleeing "WESTWARD" when their father's death exposes them to the hostility of his subjects. (It is prophetic that Siur, the most wholly sympathetic figure in the early romances, turns from unhappy love to craftsmanship and finally to revolutionary utopianism.)

The point is not that these stories reflect actual events in Morris' life, but rather that the role he most often projects for himself is that of the betrayed, renounced, or otherwise hopeless lover, whose safest recourse is to remain in the background while other men win fame and passion. "Golden Wings," in which the young outsider steals the betrothed of the older, proven warrior, substantiates Morris' fear of projecting his own erotic fulfillment. Lionel's gratified desire results in civil war and the inglorious destruction both of himself and of his bride. Similarly, in "A Dream," the lovers are separated by a girl's whim and condemned to centuries of purgatorial separation.

The version of this theme in "Frank's Sealed Letter," the only one of the early romances placed in a contemporary setting, suggests why Morris was well-advised to cast the others in an earlier period. Its setting in the environs of Walthamstow, its first-person narrative, and its hero's vocation are an exception to Morris' usual strategy of treating personal feelings with distance and indirection. The story is trite, sentimental, and self-pitying. The outcast poet-lover (Hugh) is physically deformed and ugly, and his femme fatale (Mabel!) spurns him with the unmitigated cruelty of high melodrama: "What do I want better than you? Why, I want a man who is brave and beautiful; you are a coward and cripple" (I, 311–12). Certainly nowhere else in Morris' writing is the reader faced with so embarrassing a sense of the author's self-commiseration. Even so, the narrator's opening remarks are a fair reflection of Morris' view of himself at the beginning of manhood, and as such summarize the two conflicting elements in his personality we have traced in the romances:

> Ever since I can remember, even when I was quite a child, people have always told me that I had no perseverance, no strength of will; they have always kept on saying to me, directly and indirectly: "Unstable as water, thou shalt not excel;" and they have always been quite wrong in this matter, for of all men I have heard of, I have the strongest will for good and evil. I could soon find out whether a thing were possible or not to me; then if it were not I threw it away for ever, never thought of it again; no regret, no longing for that; it was past and over to me. But if it were possible, and I made up my mind to do it, then and there I began it, and in due time finished it, turning neither to the right hand nor to the left till it was done. So I did with all things that I set my hand to. (I, 309)

The story goes on to argue that "Love only, and the wild restless passions that went with it, were too strong" for the narrator. But the fantasy of unrequited love implies something very different—Morris' fear of his own inadequacy as a lover. And Frank's recourse— "proving himself" as a writer—suggests a motivation more like Cleon's aesthetic detachment than Childe Roland's "doing his duty."

II The Defence of Guenevere and Other Poems (1858)

The poems for which Morris is best known today met with least immediate recognition. Despite a few favorable reviews, response to *The Defence of Guenevere* was generally hostile.[2] Morris' style was "bad as bad can be," and his medieval subject matter "devotion to a false principle of art." But the chief objection to *The Defence* was its author's alliance with Pre-Raphaelitism. Having dedicated the book to Rossetti, Morris found his own poetry blamed for the faults—real or imagined—of Rossetti's work and personality.[3] In fact, Rossetti's influence was comparatively slight. Swinburne, not Rossetti, encouraged Morris to complete the volume, and the style and subject matter of the poems derive from a period before Morris' acquaintance with the artist. There is more justice in the reviewers' criticism of Morris' style. But the poems' obscurities and abrupt transitions are not unrelated to their stark power. And in the dramatic monologues a certain awkwardness of meter and sound seems to verify the over-wrought emotions of the speakers.[4]

Contrasting Morris' treatment of Arthurian legend in *The Defence* with Tennyson's "Sir Galahad," Richard Garnett argued that "the difference between the two poets obviously is that Tennyson writes of mediaeval things like a modern, and Mr. Morris like a contemporary."[5] Certainly the unflinching depiction of sexuality and death that accounts for the poems' appeal to modern readers carried Morris more than once past the borderline of Victorian taste. And it is no accident that the poems most offensive to the literary establishment were the ones most prized by Morris' younger admirers. *The Defence of Guenevere* is self-consciously avant-garde poetry, and never again in his literary career did Morris show quite so much daring.

The poems in the volume fall into three categories. Those based on Arthurian materials—four of which, including the title poem, begin the collection—and the larger group based on Froissart's *Chronicles* are predominantly realistic. The third group, loosely described as "fantasies," are less easily characterized, although they share a deliberate antirealism. All three groups rely heavily on the dramatic method. Many are monologues, others contain several speaking characters. Doubtless Morris was influenced by Browning in his choice of this form, but there is no confusing the work of the two poets. The strong, often violent immediacy of the *Defence of Guenevere* poems—a quality they share with the *Oxford and Cambridge Magazine* romances—renders them unmistakeably his own.

Recent interpretations of "The Defence of Guenevere" suggest both the compelling force of the poem and the general obscurity of its argument.[6] Just what constitutes Guenevere's "Defence" is never certain. Her long address to the knights, headed by Gauwaine, who intend to execute her as an adultress can be read as an impassioned plea for understanding, as the partly defensive, partly confessional ramblings of a woman in emotional shock, or simply as a means of stalling until Lancelot arrives to the rescue. This ambiguity can be blamed on Morris. His Guenevere is confusing because he was unable to sort out his conflicting attitudes toward her. Attracted by her egoistical vitality, he nevertheless cannot wholly absolve her guilt. But the confusions of the poem also mirror the unresolved complexities of Guenevere herself. She, like Morris, is not sure whether to be proud or ashamed, to ask for sympathy or give defiance.

Loosely based on material in books 18–20 of Malory's *Morte Darthur*, the monologue begins with a rhetorical strategy that has

troubled many interpreters. "Suppose your time were come to die,"
Guenevere requests her listeners, and made to choose between two
cloths, one "heaven," and the other "hell":

> "And one of these strange choosing cloths was blue,
> Wavy and long, and one cut short and red;
> No man could tell the better of the two.
>
> "After a shivering half-hour you said:
> 'God help! heaven's colour, the blue;' and he said, 'hell.'
> Perhaps you then would roll upon your bed,
>
> "And cry to all good men that loved you well,
> 'Ah Christ! if only I had known, known, known.' "
>
> (I, 2)

Traditionally, the fair-seeming blue cloth has been identified with
Lancelot. But a recent commentator argues that "heaven's colour" is
more appropriately associated with Arthur and that Guenevere is
making the point that her marriage itself has been the hell she was
deceived into choosing.[7]

What matters, of course, is not whether it is Arthur or Lancelot she
blames for damnation, but that she attempts to disavow the responsibility for her own moral decision. Underlying this attempt is Guenevere's persistent awareness of herself as a sensuous rather than a
rational being. Her opening gestures confront us with a deeply
physical creature, and the "passionate twisting of her body" with
which Guenevere accompanies her plea for understanding is as much
a personal mannerism as an overt attempt to arouse the sexual
responses of her accusers. Metaphors come naturally to the woman
because her consciousness is innately physical. Her oblique account
of falling in love with Lancelot is a descent "slowly down some path
worn smooth and even . . . until one surely reached the sea at last."
The seasons themselves are active forces compelling her sexual
surrender. The Christmas of their first meeting gives way inexorably
to "April sunshine . . . Made awful with black hail-clouds." "And in
the Summer I grew white with flame, / And bowed my head down."

The climaxing episode in the first section of the poem is a
remarkable garden scene in which Guenevere finds herself "half mad
with beauty":

"if I had

> "Held out my long hand up against the blue,
> And, looking on the tenderly darken'd fingers,
> Thought that by rights one ought to see quite through,
>
> "There, see you, where the soft light yet lingers,
> Round by the edges; what should I have done,
> If this had joined with yellow spotted singers,
>
> "And startling green drawn upward by the sun?
> But shouting, loosed out, see now! all my hair,
> And trancedly stood watching the west wind run
>
> "With faintest half-heard breathing sound—why there
> I lose my head e'en now in doing this"
>
> (I, 4–5)

Surely part of the problem here is the vagueness of Morris' expression.[8] But this moment of reverie in which Guenevere loses awareness of the boundary between herself and the natural world prepares us for her giving way to desire,

> "When both our mouths went wandering in one way,
> And aching sorely, met among the leaves;
> Our hands being left behind strained far away."
>
> (I, 5)

"Hands" and "mouths" cease to be organs of any recognizably composite body. Guenevere herself is powerless to resist a passion unrelated to the possibility of a moral consciousness. As a representative of "sense," she is comparable to the central figure of Tennyson's "Guinevere" (completed in the same month Morris published *The Defence of Guenevere*). But unlike Tennyson's queen, she is incapable of recognizing the priority of "soul" and hence incapable of remorse.

Guenevere's abrupt turn to the functional refrain of the poem— "Nevertheless you, O Sir Gauwaine, lie"—breaks the spell. Whereas Tennyson's Guinevere listens to her husband's accusations in mute self-abasement, Morris' queen is articulate and retaliatory. The remainder of the monologue consists of thinly veiled threats—that "my knight" Lancelot *will* come—and transparent sophistries. Lan-

celot *was* is her bedchamber—but who is to say the reasons were not
innocent? In the very act of denying her sin, Guenevere unabashedly
savors its memory. Yet, as she asks her accusers, " 'Will you
dare, / When you have looked a little on my brow, / To say this thing is
vile?' "

Guenevere's "defence" is the irresistable force of her own will to
survive. Yet in the companion poem this will itself is overcome by
Arthur's puritan morality—and Morris's distrust of his own fascination with the queen. Largely a dialogue between Guenevere and
Lancelot, "At Arthur's Tomb" is the most difficult of the Arthurian
group. Lancelot has come to Guenevere at Glastonbury, but falls
asleep on a stone in the abbey courtyard, "not knowing it was
Arthur's" tomb. Meeting here, in the shadowy presence of the dead
king, neither figure seems totally responsible for his or her actions,
and their speeches wander free-associatively from the purpose of
their encounter. "Dazed" by his fatiguing journey, Lancelot recollects a night with Guenevere when he " 'fell asleep / In spite of all my
striving' "—just as he falls compulsively asleep on Arthur's tomb.
Guenevere's consciousness of guilt comes to her in the half-light of
"morning twilight, when the grey downs bare / Grew into lumps of
sin." Accused, in Guenevere's final outburst, of betraying the king,
Lancelot faints and awakens at the end of the poem to discover
Guenevere fled and his own " 'head and hands . . . bleeding from the
stone.' "

Both characters are uncertain as to what they want from one
another. The confused elements of their dialogue—nostalgia, rage,
desire, love, guilt, fear—mirror the moral confusion through which
they must both pass if they are to assume the saintly roles legend
attributes to them. But the nature of Guenevere's saintliness is clear
from her last speech in the poem:

> "Alas, alas! I know not what to do,
>   If I run fast it is perchance that I
> May fall and stun myself, much better so,
>   Never, never again! not even when I die."
>
> (I, 23)

Christian virtue is simply running away, and the Arthur whose
morality wins out is accurately characterized by the block of stone on
which Lancelot bruises his head.

The other pair of Arthurian poems replaces Guenevere, the

sensuous woman constrained by a morality she cannot understand, with Galahad, the spiritual man questioning the meaning of his spirituality. Morris, who found Tennyson's Sir Galahad "rather a mild youth,"[9] offers an alternative psychologically richer and morally more thought-provoking. At the opening of "Sir Galahad: A Christmas Mystery," Galahad contrasts himself, "a man of stone, / Dismal, unfriended" (I, 24), with the more worldly and—he believes—happier knights of the Round Table. His doubts are assuaged by a prophetic vision, and his vocation ostensibly confirmed by news of the failures of the other knights in quest of the Grail. Yet the events of his own successful quest fail to reflect Galahad's full identity, and we never lose a sense of him as victim.

"The Chapel in Lyoness" counters this dualism with the possibility of a synthesis between erotic fulfillment and holiness. As Sir Ozana lies dying—representative of the knights who failed in the quest on account of their sexual passion—Galahad realizes his religious songs are to no avail. He plucks a red rose, symbol of passion, and places it on Ozana's lips. The dying knight then shows him the golden hair of his mistress, which he clutches to his breast. He dies and Sir Galahad suggests that heaven itself may be the reunion of lovers:

> Ozana, shall I pray for thee?
> Her cheek is laid to thine;
> No long time hence, also I see
> Thy wasted fingers twine
>
> Within the tresses of her hair
> That shineth gloriously,
> Thinly outspread in the clear air
> Against the jasper sea.

(I, 34)

When we recall that Sir Galahad was to have been patron of the Oxford brotherhood, it is tempting to regard him as a surrogate for Morris himself. His resolution of the tensions of the earlier Arthurian poems with this vision of spiritualized eroticism suggests a strategy for Morris' coming to terms with his own sexuality. And insofar as Galahad's strategy depends on his vicarious identification with Ozana, it corresponds to Morris' attraction to women already singled out by other men and his need to treat them with the idealizing distance of Galahad's final vision.

The Froissartian peoms are Morris' account of the waning of the
Middle Ages.[10] In "The Haystack in the Floods," "Sir Peter
Harpdon's End," and "Concerning Geffray Teste Noire" the themes
of historical decay and individual frustration that link the early prose
romances are restated with grim realism and a tragic awareness of the
conflict between history and the individuals caught in its inexorable
process.

His most frequently anthologized poem, "The Haystack in the
Floods," typifies both elements. Taking the lovers Robert and Jehane
in ambush, Godmar offers Jehane the choice between untenable
alternatives: to become his paramour "this very hour" and save
Robert's life (for a time) or to refuse him, bring about Robert's
immediate murder, and be taken herself to Paris for trial by water as a
witch. Trapped between "sin and sin," she takes the respite of an
hour's delay to fall asleep.

> but she,
> Being waked at last, sigh'd quietly,
> And strangely childlike came, and said:
> "I will not."
>
> (I, 127)

Robert is "straightway" decapitated, and, after "five or six" of
Godmar's men have "beat / His head to pieces at their feet," Jehane is
turned back on the road to Paris.

The strength of the poem lies in its juxtaposition of thwarted
sexuality with "grinning" violence. At the moment of parting, the two
lovers struggle ineffectually for a last kiss:

> he tried once more
> To touch her lips; she reach'd out, sore
> And vain desire so tortured them,
> The poor grey lips, and now the hem
> Of his sleeve brush'd them.
>
> (I, 128)

Their tragedy is neither death nor the inability to achieve final
understanding, but a sexual frustration that has its counterpart in
Godmar's perverted eroticism. As one critic observes, "sadism takes
the place of orgasm" and "the murderer achieves the only sexual
pleasure available in the poem."[11]

Despite a few intrusions by the narrator, we see the action largely through Jehane's consciousness. The traumatic force of the event is conveyed in her focus on a sequence of images: "the dripping leafless woods" and her own numbed fatigue on horseback; the "old soak'd hay" behind which Godmar and his men lie in ambush and on which she will, in shock, rest her head and sleep; that sleeve brushing her lips; "the long bright blade without a flaw" gliding "from Godmar's sheath" to sever Robert's head from his body. Intensity of feeling drains the scene of intellectualizable meaning. Her decisive "I will not" is the spontaneous, "strangely childlike" gesture of a woman waking from sleep. But the very naiveté of her gesture overcomes the barriers of history and strikes us with an unforgettable immediacy.

In contrast, the leisurely development of "Sir Peter Harpdon's End" encourages a more complex view of the historical process. The poem dramatises the final episodes in the twenty-five-year-old knight's life. From the opening scene, in which Sir Peter surveys the hopelessness of commanding his undermanned, indefensible castle in Poictou, personal defeat is placed against the backdrop of English losses in France during the Hundred Years' War:

> times are changed,
> And now no longer does the country shake
> At sound of English names; our captains fade
> From off our muster-rolls . . .
> . . . .
> . . . and, over all,
> Edward the prince lies underneath the ground;
> Edward the king is dead; at Westminster
> The carvers smooth the curls of his long beard.
>
> (I, 37)

The irrevocable transmutation of living achievement into memory has begun. Moreover, political loss entails erotic frustration. Separated from his love Alice, Sir Peter speculates that "a few minutes talk had set things right," and fantasizes a scene between them that never occurred. Heroic action gives way to nostalgia for an imaginary past, nostalgia in turn to Sir Peter's mistaken belief that Alice has accepted the rumors of his disloyalty being spread by his cousin Lambert.

Lambert, the figure who epitomizes the survival-at-any-cost spirit of the new age, appears in the second scene. Attempting betrayal, he himself is taken by Sir Peter and his men—but only because Sir Peter had anticipated Lambert's duplicity and armed himself secretly for their interview. To outwit the forces that threaten the chivalric code, he must relinquish his own openness. And this lapse from honor colors Sir Peter's subsequent treatment of Lambert. Instead of killing him as a traitor, he offers him the choice between death and mutilation. There is something ugly in Lambert's choice of life with dishonor, but there is also something ugly in Sir Peter's cat-and-mouse toying with his captured opponent.

Then, abruptly, the tables are turned. Sir Peter has been captured by the French commander Guesclin, who has been persuaded by Lambert to execute his prisoner. (The normal course, nobly but ineffectually argued by Oliver Clisson, would have been to hold him for ransom.) In a grotesque scene, Lambert is allowed to taunt his old enemy. It becomes clear that clipping Lambert's ears meant his emasculation, and vindictiveness comes full circle to the "filthy beast" Lambert's perverse displacement of the object of Sir Peter's sexual desire: "For I am Alice, am right like her now, / Will you not kiss me on the lips, my love?" His fate sealed, Sir Peter weeps in the face of his enemies. Not, he shamefully equivocates, "at fear of death":

> I only wept because
> There was no beautiful lady to kiss me
> Before I died, and sweetly wish good speed
> From her dear lips. O for some lady, though
> I saw her ne'er before; Alice, my love,
> I do not ask for.
>
> (I, 53)

Erotic fulfillment is no longer a complement to chivalric honor, but a means of evading the fact of defeat. And it is no longer the knight's chosen lady he identifies with eros, but mere undifferentiated female sexuality.

Ironically, Alice herself, whose response to the news of Sir Peter's execution forms the final scene of the poem, uses sex as a similar means of evasion. Just as Sir Peter longed for the kiss of a woman to obliterate his sense of the present, Alice summons a disturbingly erotic image of Christ to save her from the full realization of her own grief.

"Concerning Geffray Teste Noire" engages a new perspective on the Froissart materials. The poem is addressed by John of Castle Neuf (alternatively, "Newcastle") to an unidentified "Alleyne," whom the narrator urges to convey his story to none other than Froissart himself ("the Canon of Chimay"). That Newcastle's story does not appear in the *Chronicles* is a framing irony for the poem. His attempt to become an "historical" figure fails, while his rival Teste Noire has a place in Froissart. But the fickleness of history is not the poem's chief message. Newcastle's account of the death of Teste Noire mediates a curiously interrelated central reminiscence. The historical frame involves his assignment with "Sir John Bonne Lance, / And other knights" to put an end to Geffray Teste Noire,

> a Gascon thief,
> Who, under shadow of the English name,
> Pilled all such towns and countries as were lief
> To King Charles and St. Dennis.

(I, 75)

Having besieged Teste Noire—ineffectually—at his stronghold at Ventadour, a party of thirty knights, including Newcastle, attempt to ambush him on the road. But Teste Noire is not among the men that waylay and slaughter, and he dies instead in his own bed "From a wound pick'd up at a barrier fray. . . . And much bad living."

Like Teste Noire himself, his adversaries are no better than robbers. The "Gascon thief" who robs "under shadow of the English name" and the narrator with interchangeable French and English surnames are two of a kind. Both live off pillage. The outcome of their struggle means nothing to the "burghers and villaynes" of the countryside, who have been preyed upon equally by both parties. Thus Teste Noire's death is less an anticlimax than an irrelevance.

What is central to Newcastle's narrative is not these mindless games of plunder, but two deeply personal and strangely connected experiences that he links with his memory of the ambush. Preparing to waylay Teste Noire, Newcastle comes across the bones of a knight and what is pointed out to him must be the knight's lady. Musing over their remains, he creates an imaginary account of their death and then, forgetting the knight, transforms the lady into the object of his own sexual desire.

Newcastle is thus another version of Sir Galahad in "The Chapel in Lyoness." However, his erotic reverie is not merely framed by the ironic brutality of the ambush, but also counterpointed by his recollection of the time when as a boy of fifteen, accompanying his father in the slaughter "with great joy" of a faction of rebellious peasants, he

> faint with smelling the burnt bones,
> And very hot with fighting down the street,
> And sick of such a life, fell down, with groans
> My head went weakly nodding to my feet.

(I, 78)

The boy's initiation into the world of adult violence is first "joy" then somatic revulsion. Similarly, the news that he is to lead the ambush makes him feel "like the horse in Job, who hears/The dancing trumpet sound." But the need to "put cloths about [his] arms,/Lest they should glitter" and "lay down [his] pennon in the grass"—that is, to exchange the code of chivalric honor for that of guerilla warfare— confronts him with the bones of the knight and lady and commences the sexual fantasy through which he recoils from the brutal present. Yet as his idealization of the Lady intensifies (through a shift into the present tense), the mutuality of love and war is increasingly explicit:

> I saw you kissing once, like a curved sword
> That bites with all its edge, did your lips lie,
> Curled gently, slowly, long time could afford
> For caught-up breathings.

(I, 80)

Romance, in other words, is no alternative to violence. Sir John can only conceive of sexual fulfillment as a form of destruction. Thus the abrupt transition from erotic reverie to the businesslike details of ambush is as natural as it is tragic.

Newcastle is trapped in a world of violence. Like Galahad, he attempts to participate in someone else's passion by an act of the imagination. He builds a monument in his chapel for the bones of the two dead lovers. But the sculptor is dead and his work, like the tomb in "The Story of the Unknown Church," has not survived. Finally, all Newcastle has won for himself is the sad awareness, "I am old."

Of the remaining lyrics and ballads in *The Defence of Guenevere,* many are akin to the longer Arthurian or Froissartian poems. But there are others that do not lend themselves to easy classification. The terms that have been used to describe them—"fantasies," "fantastic romances"[12]—are at best convenient oversimplifications. "The Wind" and "The Blue Closet" are genuinely symbolist poems, strongly evocative but irreducible in meaning. (It is a meaningful coincidence that Morris' volume was published only a year after

Baudelaire's *Fleurs du Mal* appeared in France.) Like the poetry of the French symbolists, Morris' poems are strongly influenced by Poe. Also like the symbolists, he assumes a significant relationship between poetry and painting. "The Blue Closet," one of two poems inspired by Rossetti paintings, describes a room in a tower and a room under the sea, in the past and in the present, a purgatorial memory and a glimpse of heaven. The active agents in the poem are pronouns without antecedents. In the company of her sister and "damozels," Lady Louise awaits the return of her lover, but we misread the poem if we try to fix the circumstances of his departure—or even how long ago it occurred. For reasons that remain unspecified, *this* Christmas Eve her annual song in the blue closet is answered with an image through which the mutuality of sex and death is made explicit:

> *Through the floor shot up a lily red,*
> *With a patch of earth from the land of the dead,*
> *For he was strong in the land of the dead.*
>
> (I, 113)

Superficially perceived, the fantasies may seem antithetical to the naturalistic poems in *The Defence,* but their willingness to explore the raw output of the unconscious mind is simply another aspect of Morris' psychological realism. The speaker of "The Wind"—another character waiting for an impossible return—is clearly psychotic. (The orange in the following is a design on the hangings behind his chair.)

> If I move my chair it will scream, and the orange will
>   roll out far,
> And the faint yellow juice ooze out like blood
>   from a wizard's jar;
> And the dogs will howl for those who went last month
>   to the war.
>
> (I, 107)

As in "The Blue Closet," the ghosts of the dead do, at last, return—but not the ghost of the woman he loved. There is no miraculous reunion, only painful, inconclusive recognition. The something that was to have happened turns out to be but a further stage in the mental deterioration of the speaker, whose *"derangement of all the senses"* is in keeping with the poetic creed of Arthur Rimbaud, youngest of the French symbolists.

The action of "Rapunzel," longest of the fantasy poems, is

psychological, not heroic; events occur because they are appropriate to the changing perceptions of the characters, not by material causes. By this means, the familiar fairy tale is metamorphosized into a symbolic narrative of self-discovery and erotic fulfillment. Pressed by social conventions to marry ("Thou art a king's own son, / 'Tis fit that thou should'st wed"), the prince withdraws into the dreamlike fantasy state characteristic of Morris' early heroes. Conversely, Rapunzel responds to her imprisonment in the witch's tower with a fatalism unbefitting her years ("I am growing old, / For want of love my heart is cold"). The prince awakens from his dream by recognizing that Rapunzel is a real maiden in a real tower; Rapunzel, from her fatalism by clarifying her desire in an erotic image of rescue:

> Give me a kiss,
> Dear God, dwelling up in heaven!
> Also: Send me a true knight,
> Lord Christ, with a steel sword, bright,
> Broad, and trenchant; yea, and seven
> Spans from hilt to point.

(I, 68)

The lovers are united; we learn that the prince's name is Sebald, that Rapunzel's real name is unknown ("The witch's name was Rapunzel"). Recalling the minstrel's song that induced his original fantasy, the prince gives her the name Guendolen. Their identities secure, King Sebald and Guendolen speak together *"Afterwards, in the Palace,"* while the witch's voice—plaintive or, perhaps, sinister— rises *"out of hell."*

The poem repays close attention. While its primary meaning seems to reflect a pattern of growth from the undifferentiated consciousness of childhood to adult "love and individuality,"[13] the terms of this process are not easy to agree on. Clearly the imagination has something to do with this transition. It is a song that initiates Sebald's quest and gives his love a name, and, as Dianne Sadoff argues, the stages of the lovers' development parallel the creative process itself.[14] But the poem does not draw on a consistent theory of artistic or psychological growth. Rather, one senses the poet giving himself up to the promptings of his own unconscious and allowing them to dictate the events of the narrative.

Significantly, Morris placed "Rapunzel" near the head of the collection, immediately following the four longer Arthurian poems, between "Sir Peter Harpdon's End" and "Concerning Geffray Teste

Noire." The most optimistic of the seven poems, it is clearly related to the sexual fantasies of Sir Galahad and John of Newcastle—the two characters most readily identifiable with Morris himself. As such, it suggests the possibility of working through vicarious sexual fantasy to genuine erotic fulfillment by transforming the figure of the prior rival into that of a dominant older woman. "Rapunzel" is thus a positive sign in Morris' psychological development and foreshadows the healthy sexuality of the late romances.

CHAPTER 3

"A Shadowy Isle of Bliss": Jason and The Earthly Paradise

NEARLY a decade lapsed between the publication of *The Defence of Guenevere* in 1858 and *The Life and Death of Jason* and the first volume of *The Earthly Paradise* in 1867 and 1868. During this period much had occurred in Morris' life. He had given up his career as a painter and had found a new challenge in the work of Morris and Company. He had built, lived in, and moved away from Red House. He had fallen in love, married, and by the mid 1860s begun to sense the deterioration of his married life. "The author of *The Earthly Paradise*"—as Morris came to be known by the reading public—was thus a man considerably altered from the poet of *The Defence of Guenevere*. He was a man who had experienced change and failure—in particular the failure of love. He was, consequently, a man who had come to recognize the self-destructiveness of his own passion. Yet he was also a man unwilling to deny the strength and significance of human desire: on the one hand, a man characterized by despair and resignation; on the other, by the staunch affirmation of his own erotic and creative drives. For Morris this emotional division was not a standoff; rather, it provided the terms of a dialectical process—a process central both to his psychological development and, by extension, to the narrative poetry of *The Earthly Paradise*.

I *The Narrative Frame of* The Earthly Paradise

The plan of *The Earthly Paradise* is simple. A group of aged seafarers from Northern Europe ("the Wanderers") arrive at a long-lost Greek colony in the Atlantic where during the ensuing year they meet to banquet and exchange stories with the Elders of the City. Each group contributes a story a month; thus the poem is divided into twelve months, each month into two stories, one classical, one medieval. However this simple format is complicated by the double framework of a pseudohistorical account of the storytellers and Morris' enclosing commentary on the poem as a whole. The contrast between this elaborately mediated structure and the dramatic straightforwardness of *The Defence of Guenevere* marks an abrupt redirection in Morris' work. In part this redirection derives from the unsuitability of the dramatic technique for extended narratives with multiple characters. (Morris discovered this in his abortive "Scenes from the Fall of Troy," begun and laid aside early in the 1860s.) But more important, the earlier mode did not offer Morris the self-expression he seems to have sought. In *The Earthly Paradise* he found his identity as a storyteller.

Preparing a collection of medieval stories, it was only natural for Morris to turn to Chaucer as a model, but the frame of *The Earthly Paradise* serves a very different function from that of *The Canterbury Tales*. Not merely are Morris' characters presumed to have lived five hundred years before the poet himself, but he is not concerned with presenting them *as* characters. Largely undifferentiated from one another, they exist primarily as a means for Morris to isolate the simple narrative of the twenty-four traditional stories from the complex, often highly personal meditations of the nineteenth-century poet.

Morris' voice is most differentiated from that of his characters in the lyrics that head the twelve monthly sections. Ostensibly his reflections on the changing landscape, they treat his deteriorating relationship with an unspecified "love"—doubtless Jane—who appears in the May, July, August, October, and January poems. Despite their correspondence with the cycle of the year, the lyrics portray a man profoundly alienated from the sources of emotional rebirth. The words "death," "dead," or "die" occur in eight of the twelve poems. The hopefulness of Spring is undercut by his "fear" of the coming summer (III, 169). The "kindness" of June is at best a "rare happy dream" from which he knows he will waken (IV, 87). "The thought of glorious Summer lives" yet in August, but their "happy days" are wasted in "craving for the best, / Like lovers o'er the painted images / Of those who once their yearning hearts have blessed" (IV, 187). On the other hand, the "new-awakened man" of September can only try "To dream again the dream that made him glad" (V, 1). For "the real world" of Morris' November vision is a "strange image of the dread Eternity" in which he can perceive no place for "These outstretched feverish hands, this restless heart" (V,

206). With the passing of the old year, December grants him a qualified—conventional—hope for the future, and January allows him a glimpse of the "scarce-seen kindly smile" of his beloved (VI, 65). But this unexpected moment of communication simply intensifies his awareness of loss, and February, instead of promising renewed life, ends with an unanswered question: "Shalt thou not hope for joy new born again,/Since no grief ever born can ever die/Through changeless change of seasons passing by?" (VI, 175). Thus, the passing of the year does not heal grief nor even divert Morris from his melancholy; it merely commemorates the permanence of despair.

This split between man and the natural world is essential to *The Earthly Paradise*. Not only is nature unable to satisfy or assuage human passion, the imagination is also incapable of reshaping objective reality to its own purposes. These limitations confront us directly in the string of disclaimers that open "The Apology":

> Of Heaven or Hell I have no power to sing,
> I cannot ease the burden of your fears,
> Or make quick-coming death a little thing,
> Or bring again the pleasure of past years,
> Nor for my words shall ye forget your tears,
> Or hope again for aught that I can say,
> The idle singer of an empty day.
>
> (III, 1)

In these opening lines of *The Earthly Paradise* Morris' need to control the personal anxiety that underlies his storytelling has already organized itself into a bold gesture of poetic identity. Assuming the role of "idle singer" is neither an act of humility nor a rejection of his own age. Rather, Morris is liberating himself from the demands of public responsibility and private sincerity that were the legacy of the romantics to their successors in the later nineteenth century. The "empty day" of which Morris proclaims himself the "idle singer" is neither the moral nor aesthetic void of Victorian England nor simply the "mood of idleness" Blue Calhoun associates with the pastoral.[1] Rather, it is the demythologized perception of nature Morris believed necessary for the revitalization of English poetry.

The "murmuring rhyme" Morris promises will convey "a tale not too importunate/To those who in the sleepy regions stay" hits us where we are most vulnerable—at the moment between sleep and wakening when judgment is suspended and the categories of perception unregulated. But Morris' description of himself as a "Dreamer of Dreams" is superceded by a more accurate representation of the poet's craft he aimed at:

> Folk say, a wizard to a northern king
> At Christmas-tide such wondrous things did show,
> That through one window men beheld the spring,
> And through another saw the summer glow,
> And through a third the fruited vines a-row,
> While still, unheard, but in its wonted way,
> Piped the drear wind of the December day.
>
> So with this Earthly Paradise it is,
> If ye will read aright, and pardon me,
> Who strive to build a shadowy isle of bliss
> Midmost the beating of the steely sea.

(III, 2)

The basis of the wizard's art is the zero vision of winter. His illusions can divert us from "the drear wind," but the diversion cannot change reality. To "read aright," then, is not to escape, but to recognize the fundamental chasm between the real and the imagined and, as a consequence, the fundamental daring of the imagination in—temporarily—overcoming its limitations.

Attaining this disciplined state of mind is the achievement of the Wanderers' quest. "A nameless city in a distant sea,/White as the changing walls of faërie" (III, 3), the Greek colony defines the conditions under which the peculiar art of *The Earthly Paradise* can flourish: apparently timeless continuity with the past; tenuous detachment from the "business" of the modern world; a strong awareness of its own limitations—here, the geographical boundaries of the "shadowy isle of bliss" itself. Moreover, this locus for creativity is not an ivory tower, cut off from the real world, such as Tennyson described in "The Palace of Art," but a social organism; its art, not the expression of an individual, but of popular tradition.

As narrators, the Wanderers and their hosts are spokesmen for their two cultural heritages. They are essentially naive, in contrast to the first-person poet, whose ironic awareness of the disjunction between past and present suggests the attitude a modern reader will perforce take to their storytelling. But this division between past and present, ironic and naive is in itself too drastic. It implies an unresolvable split between the elements of Morris' creative personality. What is needed is the affirmation of a common ground for the two voices, and this Morris achieves through the prologue. Rolf, its main narrator, shares the naiveté of his companions, but also the self-consciousness of the nineteenth-century narrator. As a result, his story, unlike the twenty-four tales that follow, is a distinctly modern poem, through which Morris is able to explore the limitations of his own creative mind.

Rolf tells the Elders how, as a young man, he had fled plague-ridden Norway, along with two companions—the Breton Nicholas and Laurence, a Swabian priest and alchemist—and the crews of two ships, in quest of "gardens ever blossoming/Across the Western Sea where none grew old" (III, 7). Their adventures occur in a geographically uncertain version of the New World, where they come first upon a society of forest-dwellers, "of all the folk I ever saw . . . the gentlest" (III, 37), who honor them as beings of a superior order. But this people's primitive innocence fails to satisfy the Wanderers, who resume their voyage. After a brief episode in which they are attacked by hostile savages (the alternative form of primitivism), they encounter a second group of hospitable aborigines, "nigh void of arts, but harmless, good, and mild," who tell them of a land "o'er the mountains . . . Where folk dwelt, clothed and armed like us" (III, 44), which the Wanderers assume to be the Earthly Paradise they seek. They winter with the "harmless" people, learning each other's language and lore. But when spring comes, Rolf addresses his companions—much in the style of Tennyson's Ulysses—urging them to resume the quest. Significantly, some refuse, preferring to live the "dull life" of primitive society as a just reward for the folly of setting forth on a hopeless voyage. Thus, the alternatives are sharpened, the body of questers reduced. Ironically, the men "like to us" on the other side of the mountains turn out to be cannibals, fighting with whom the Wanderers themselves "grew like devils" (III, 49). Returning to their companions "yet alive and well,/Wedded to brown wives" (III, 49–50), the two-score remaining questers resume their voyage and, after various encounters with more primitive societies—"some . . . dangerous and some . . . kind" (III, 52)—reach a more advanced culture where, once again, they are received as gods. So honored, they pass many years. Yet with the coming of middle age, Rolf and his closest companions again hunger after the quest they have lain aside. Deceived by a trumped-up show of rejuvenation, they are taken prisoner and taunted by their captors in a demonic parody of their own quest: " 'O ye, who sought to find/Unending life against the law of kind . . . ye are our gods on earth/Whiles that ye live . . . ah, surely ye are come,/When all is said, unto an envied home' " (III, 72). But in time their captors are overwhelmed by an enemy, and, as the city burns, the Wanderers flee, setting sail on the voyage that will eventually take them to the Hellenic island on which the narratives take place.

What is immediately striking about this account is its repetitive structure, and this pattern of repetition is all the more remarkable when the published prologue is compared to the version of the story Morris originally intended to introduce *The Earthly Paradise*. The earlier poem is a symbolic narrative of guilt and retribution—strongly influenced by Coleridge's *Rime of the Ancient Mariner*—in which the Wanderers' quest is a gesture of hubris—"Adam's sin/To make us Gods who are but men" (XXIV, 110); their heroism, gratuitous brutality. In contrast with the clear-cut allegory of the first version, the moral terms of the revised prologue are considerably less certain, and its pattern of repetition suggests that it is not a single act but a consistent attitude toward life that constitutes the meaning of the Wanderers' quest.

In addition to their emphasis on repetition, Morris' revisions entail two general trends: an increasingly realist account of the details of the voyage and an increasingly positive view of the quest itself. In the first version, the Wanderers set off in response to a dream. In the second, their motivations include the plague and, as Blue Calhoun points out, the breakup of medieval civilization.[2] Moreover, their goal has the sanction of traditional legend and arcane study. Thus they are exemplars of the same historical forces that propelled Europeans to the Americas.[3] And these revisions transform the Wanderers from the guilty protagonists of an impossible fantasy into possible figures in a largely possible narrative. The Wanderers of the 1868 prologue are men with whom Morris the poet can identify and whose quest as a consequence becomes a functional analogue to his own search for imaginative and erotic fulfillment.

Among the new material in the second prologue, one episode is particularly important in revaluing the Wanderers' quest. Passing through the English channel, they encounter Edward III on his way to war with France. The English king offers to take them into his service, and Rolf wavers. But Nicholas prevents him from deserting the quest with a long speech in which he sets forth their aims. It is death—not just the plague, but the fact of human experience—they flee. And it is Nicholas' very love of "this changing life of men" and the "bliss" of "every minute" (III, 20) that precipitates their flight. The questers of the old prologue sought a new state of being; the questers of the later poem search for the permanence of a world they know, love, and—were it not for its transcience—find totally adequate to their desires. And it is because they seek fulfillment *within* nature that they are capable of attaining an awareness of its limitations. Ironically, the 1865–1866 Wanderers were chastened by the providential order of the very natural world they sought to escape. But it is the absence of anything in nature akin to Providence that the Wanderers of the 1868 prologue must bring themselves to realize.

Edward, too, has come to doubt the heroic code. But unlike the Wanderers his response is a mixture of resigned pragmatism and conventional religiosity. Thus the encounter between Edward and the Wanderers enables Morris to juxtapose the alternative responses to cultural disintegration. So conceived, the thrust of the episode is not toward a judgment of either response, but toward a recognition of the difficulty of choosing between them. But while Morris was unprepared in 1868 to side wholly with the Wanderers, the epilogue he wrote to the final volume of *The Earthly Paradise* (1870) acknowledges his identification with their quest:

> Surely on their side I at least will be,
> And deem that when at last, their fear worn out,
> They fell asleep, all that old shame and doubt,
> Shamed them not now, nor did they doubt it good,
> That they in arms against that Death had stood.
>
> (VI, 329)

Morris is able to make this identification with the Wanderers because their quest was a failure. For their voyage is not merely the subject of art, it is a gesture equivalent to the artist's creative daring, meaningful because its imaginative bravura is just as tenuous, just as limited as the poet's "shadowy isle of bliss." Appropriately, the Wanderers appear to sense this at the moment they believe themselves closest to success:

> And not in vain our former joy we thought,
> Since thirty years our wandering feet have brought
> To this at last—and yet, what will you have?
> Can man be made content? We wished to save

> The bygone years; our hope, our painted toy,
> We feared to miss, drowned in that sea of joy.

(III, 67–68)

The Wanderers are not just afraid to lose memory; they fear to lose the memory of hope. For hope is the awareness of their own imaginative daring. Rightly, they fear that the achievement of their quest will render them lesser men than they were when they acted *in spite of* the fear they were undertaking the impossible.

Balancing hope with resignation, romantic individualists alienated from their cultural heritage, the Wanderers are Morris' ideal storytellers. Yet they, like the "shadowy isle" on which their storytelling takes place, betray a fundamental unsureness in Morris' attitude toward his own work. Despite its psychological usefulness, the fact that they are not realized characters but strategies for detaching Morris from responsibility for his poetry is a crucial weakness in *The Earthly Paradise*. And the unresolved tension between realistic detail and fantasy in his account of the Greek island suggests Morris' reluctance to commit himself fully to the narrative art it fosters. Yet if the frame of *The Earthly Paradise* does not resolve the difficulties Morris faced as a poet, it should awaken us to the genuine and fruitful complexities of the poem as a whole.

II   The Life and Death of Jason *(1867)*

According to May Morris, her father had planned "The Deeds of Jason" to head the twenty-four *Earthly Paradise* stories. It would thus have immediately followed the prologue—representing, in effect, the Elders' response to the story of the Wanderers' quest—and this position explains much about the longer work into which the shorter "Deeds" poem evolved. Like the *Earthly Paradise* stories, *The Life and Death of Jason* presents the classical past through the eyes of the Middle Ages. Book 17 even opens with an invocation to his "Master Chaucer," in which Morris suggests that *Troilus and Criseyde* is his model. Yet he deliberately postpones this invocation until the final book of the poem—the only section at all comparable to Chaucer's romance—and on the whole the medieval element is less strong in *Jason* than it is in the twelve classical stories of *The Earthly Paradise*. The strong simplicity of his narrative seems to confront us with primary myth, and his use of epithets, heroic similes, and various epic conventions—the catalog of Argonauts in book 3, the "machin-

ery" of gods and goddesses, Juno's special patronage of Jason—
suggest that Morris was attempting to write a romantic epic in the
manner of his chief source, the third-century B.C. *Argonautica* of
Apollonius of Rhodes, rather than a medieval romance.[4]

This contrast between Hellenistic and medieval genres functions
through certain overall similarities between *Jason* and the prologue
to *The Earthly Paradise*. Like "The Wanderers," Jason is the story of
an extended voyage. Like the Wanderers, the Argonauts find
themselves confronting an unexplored territory (Eastern Europe)
inhabited by aboriginal cultures and primitive biological forms. And
like *The Earthly Paradise* itself, the Argonauts' adventures are
dominated by the changing seasons of a single year. But, in contrast to
"The Wanderers," *Jason* recounts a voyage with two distinct and
successfully attained purposes—securing the Golden Fleece and
returning with it to Greece. Hence, the Argonauts' voyage is not a
wandering line, but a circle returning to the point of its origin.
Significantly, the Argonauts achieve their goals by rejecting a
sequence of real or apparent Earthly Paradises, and it is through this
pattern that the opposition between the two works is clearest.

Even before the quest, Jason is induced to leave the Saturnian
forest-world ("like to the golden-age"—II, 4) where he was brought
up by the centaur Chiron. The very moment he prepares to seize the
Fleece, Jason muses on this choice:

> "Too late to fear, it was too late, the hour
> I left the grey cliffs and the beechen bower,
> So here I take hard life and deathless praise,
> Who once was fain of nought but quiet days,
> And painless life, not empty of delight."
>
> (II, 130)

As for the narrator of "The Wanderers," the choice lies between
deeds and timeless indolence. Unlike Rolf, Jason chooses deeds, and
the success of his quest would seem to validate his decision. Again
and again the poem suggests that men were not meant for life in an
Earthly Paradise, and that apparent Paradises are not to be trusted.

Aea, where the Fleece is held, strikes the newly arrived Argonauts
as "an earthly Paradise," but they "looked to find sharp ending to
their bliss" (II, 99). Similarly, Circe's magic island is a trap—more
Spenserian in inspiration than Homeric—safe only for her niece
Medea to enter. Even the sight of the Garden of the Hesperides is

dangerous. "Depart in haste," its guardians warn, "for your eyes, grown over-bold, / Your hearts shall pay in sorrowing, / For want of many a half-seen thing" (II, 209). Their garden is "a place not made for earthly bliss, / Or eyes of dying man" (II, 207).

> "Nay, rather let them find their life
> Bitter and sweet, fulfilled of strife,
> Restless with hope, vain with regret,
> Trembling with fear, most strangely set
> 'Twixt memory and forgetfulness."
>
> (II, 211)

The alternative to this prelapsarian paradise is thus not simply the life of action, but the pervasive dualism of a world in which success and failure, joy and sorrow are inextricably combined.

Accordingly, it is fitting that Medea destroys Pelias by convincing him and his daughters that she knows the secret of rejuvenation. Her strategem resembles the ruse by which the Wanderers are taken prisoner in the penultimate episode of their voyage. But Pelias' reasoning suggests the self-delusion exorcised from the 1868 prologue:

> "If indeed I might not die,
> Then would I lay aside all treachery,
> And here should all folk live without alarm,
> For to no man would I do any harm,
> Whatso might hap, but I would bring again
> The golden age, free from all fear and pain."
>
> (II, 225)

But the poem's strongest rejection of an Earthly Paradise occurs in Orpheus' extended song contest with the Sirens. Luring the Argonauts to their treacherous shore, the Sirens promise a "land where none grows old, / And none is rash or over-bold . . . No vain desire of unknown things" (II, 202). Orpheus counters with an explicit denial of the Wanderers' goal:

> Ah! do ye weary of the strife
> And long to change this eager life
> For shadowy and dull hopelessness,

"there to die and not to die . . . Yet keep your memory fresh and

green," he asks—then answers his own question, arguing that
memory itself requires active participation in the cycles of nature:

> the sweet flower-scented wind,
> The dew, the gentle rain at night,
> The wonder-working snow and white,
> The song of birds, the water's fall,
> The sun that maketh bliss of all;
> Yea, this our toil and victory,
> The tyrannous and conquered sea.

(II, 203–4)

This affirmation of the earthly links *Jason* with the conclusion of the
1865–1866 "Wanderers." But like the 1868 prologue, *Jason* is an
ambiguous poem. When Hylas is seduced by nymphs into a state of
being very much like that the Sirens offer, Juno tells the Argonauts

> "he praises Jove that he was born,
> Forgetting the rough world, and every care;
> Not dead, nor living, among faces fair,
> White limbs and wonders of the watery world."

(II, 73)

Does a different logic apply here because the underwater paradise of
the nymphs is real, while that of the Sirens was merely an enticement
to death? If so, then the significance of Orpheus' song is itself called
into question. On the other hand, is this simply Juno's view of the
affair?

Moreover, even Orpheus is not entirely consistent in his affirma-
tions of the here-and-now. In book 10 the Argonauts pause in the
wilds of Russia to feast, "And all the kings being satisfied in
turn,/With vain desires 'gan their hearts to burn" (II, 150). Orpheus
counters this undirected and therefore unappeaseable lust for action
with a song lamenting the loss of " 'Saturn's days of gold.' " Now
only "song" itself, he avers, " 'may change our tuneless moan,' "

> "the unnamed smouldering fire
> Within our hearts turns to desire
> Sweet, amorous, half satisfied."

(II, 152)

Orpheus' song, like the poetry of *The Earthly Paradise*, recreates the
myth of a golden age in order to give form to the indeterminate

dissatisfaction of the Argonauts. He creates "desire," which by the very act of being brought into consciousness is "half satisfied." Thus, as in "The Apology" to *The Earthly Paradise*, art is made to compensate for the insufficiency of deeds.

However, it is neither Hylas nor Orpheus who establishes the significant irony of the poem. Before he can return to Thessaly, Jason must atone for the death of Medea's brother by offering sacrifice on Cape Malea, the first Greek soil they reach on their homeward journey. Here, at the moment of their triumph, Morris ominously describes

> The mighty voices of the Minyae
> Exulting o'er the tossing conquered sea,
> That far below thrust on by tide and wind
> The crumbling bases of the headland mined.
>
> (II, 213)

Success within the world of heroic action entails subjugation to the continual forces of natural decay. And so Jason's betrayal of Medea, the death of Glaucé, and his own death provide a necessary pendant to the heroic quest for the Golden Fleece.

Appropriately it is in the invocation to this concluding section of the poem that Morris alludes to *Troilus and Criseyde*. The classical *Jason* ends "in happy days, and rest, and peace" (II, 259). Its medieval pendant is one more example of the inexorable fall of great men. Just as the Wanderers' late medieval quest is placed in perspective by their encounter with classical civilization, the voyage of Jason is reappraised in terms of a medieval notion of tragedy.

If *The Life and Death of Jason* is a less attractive poem than "The Wanderers," it is largely because the anticlimactic structure of *Jason* necessarily undercuts the stature of the hero. Unlike the Wanderers, who grew in Morris' esteem as he wrote the poem, Jason never fully engaged Morris' imagination. And so his revaluation of the Wanderers' quest has its counterpart in his dissatisfaction with the classical man of action he originally intended to serve as a foil for the Wanderers' folly.

May Morris was probably right when she argued that her "father's sympathies were with Medea—not Medea the sorceress, but the woman weak in the very strength of her love; that he found the hero himself rather second-rate" (II, xvi). The tragic heroine whose magic both aids her lover and alienates him from her, Medea prefigures what was to become a central image in Morris' late romances.

However, here he is not quite sure how to handle her. He revises or tones down the episodes in which she is excessively brutal—the death of her brother (which he attributes to Jason) and the murder of her children. Yet he allows her to slip from the story at the very time the reader's interest in her fate has been quickened. Morris was not ready—or perhaps willing—to come to terms with a character capable of acting out her revenge in such violent terms. Nevertheless, Medea is clearly a being who kindled his fascination and as such she accounts in large part for the enduring interest of the poem.

III   The Earthly Paradise: *Spring and Summer*

The storytelling that displaces the geographical paradise of the Wanderers' quest focuses almost exclusively on the theme of erotic fulfillment. Twenty of the twenty-four tales, eleven of the final twelve, deal with romantic love, and Carole Silver rightly argues that "it is on these patterns rather than the physical quest for a terrestrial Eden that *The Earthly Paradise* is really centered."[5] But her view that "Morris seeks a nostrum in the experience of romantic love, only to contend that love too fails to make a heaven on earth" is an inadequate representation of the poem. The Elders become artists by maintaining an unbroken link with the past; the Wanderers, through dogged adherence to its rejection. One art is a function of participation in a culture; the other, of the alienated sensibilities of its creators. Given this scheme, love can be seen alternatively as the reward society grants its heroes or the self-defining gesture of the romantic lover. With few exceptions, the first is the perspective of the Elders, the second of the Wanderers.

But for the Wanderers—and for Morris himself—erotic fulfillment is not just a remedy for failure. It is also an expansion of the significance of their quest. Eros is not a substitute for but an analogue to the geographical search for an Earthly Paradise—although in a story like "The Land East of the Sun and West of the Moon" the two themes are interchangeable. Both are attempts of the human spirit to shape the world in its own image. Thus it would be wrong to read *The Earthly Paradise* as an arbitrary collection of stories. (So perceived, the basic similarity of the tales is merely monotonous.) Instead, their recurrent themes and characters must be experienced as a rhythmn through which the imagination expands and contracts its energies. Similarity becomes sustained recurrence; the power of the creative mind is perceived as process rather than product.

This rhythm develops through two structural patterns—the ordering by months and the pairing of individual narratives within each of the twelve sections. This calendrical arrangement at once subordinates the modes of the twenty-four stories within an inclusive system—roughly correlated with the four seasons—and suggests their universality as recurrent states of human experience. By adhering to the "natural" year of earlier calendars and beginning the cycle with March, Morris establishes a pattern leading inexorably from birth through maturation and harvest to death. In keeping with this pattern, the spring and summer stories—originally published as a single volume—express a constellation of positive values. They reflect the time of beginnings, of innocence, of hope, of young love and untainted heroism, of social integration and generally uncomplicated morality. Within the dialectical sequence of paired narratives, Morris' treatment of these values evolves from the relative simplicity of the earliest stories to the heightened awareness of the summer tales, in which the very ripeness of his vision calls out for its antithesis. And his erotic questers grow from the two-dimensional figures of myth to complex, self-conscious human beings.

The first of the two March stories, "Atalanta's Race," establishes an archetype of the virgin rescued by a hero from the dominance of a father-figure that is recurrent in the later stories. Morris' "Argument" summarizes the legend: "Atalanta, daughter of King Schoeneus, not willing to lose her virgin's estate, made it a law to all suitors that they should run a race with her in the public place, and if they failed to overcome her should die unrevenged; and thus many brave men perished. At last came Milanion, the son of Amphidamas, who, outrunning her with the help of Venus, gained the virgin and wedded her" (III, 85). Abandoned in infancy by a father who " 'had vowed to leave but men alone/Sprung from his loins' " and brought up in the forest by " 'a rough root-grubbing bear' " (III, 89), Atalanta's vow to Diana is a symptom of the father fixation through which she has reacted to this early rejection, and the race itself confirms her identification with a masculine role. But by the time the tale opens the blocking figure of Schoeneus has tired of the ritual slaughter, and his subjects are growing restive in face of the apparently endless decapitations. Even Venus, who plays a more ambivalent role in the later narratives, comes freely to Melanion's aid and gives him the three golden apples—symbols of fecundity—he tosses before Atalanta each of the three times she is overcoming him in the race.

Milanion has everyone on his side but Atalanta herself, and she is not so much an enemy as a creature as yet unawakened to human emotion.

Wedding Atalanta, Milanion not only fulfills his erotic quest. He also forestalls the potential disorder of Schoeneus' kingdom. Thus, in the first of the spring tales love and political expediency are interactive components of the hero's success. And this interaction is also present in the Wanderers' March story, "The Man Born to Be King." Warned by a sage that his reign will be followed by that of a man "low-born and poor," and directed to the boy himself by a dream, the king makes a series of attempts to avert fate by killing his successor. Cast adrift on a river, the infant is found and reared by a miller and his wife. Left wounded in a forest, the young man is rescued by monks. Finally, sent with a letter commanding that its bearer be put to death, Michael is discovered sleeping in a garden by the king's daughter, who substitutes a letter instructing their marriage. Confronted with the happy couple, the king resigns himself to the fate he had so long tried to escape and names Michael his successor.

As in "Atalanta's Race," circumstances conspire for the success of the hero and heroine. But while "Atalanta's Race" is told from the perspective of Milanion, "The Man Born to Be King" focuses on the negative figure of the king. As a consequence, the tale is not merely an account of fulfilled love, but a parable on the folly of attempting to avert destiny. " 'What joy of well-accomplished days,/If I had let these things alone,' " muses the King at the end of the story, " 'Nor sought to sit upon my throne/Like God between the cherubim' " (III, 167).

In these early stories eros is opposed to the effort to dominate natural process. And the attempt to restrain process is allowed to result only in static lifelessness or outright bloodshed. Instead of affirming his power, it alienates the figure of dominance from the sources of psychological and political stability. Atalanta's chastity answers to her father's desire for a male child, but only at the cost of human sacrifice Schoeneus himself is glad to bring to an end. The king's efforts to murder his fated successor merely heighten his own insecurity and prepare the boy to assume kingship. Love, on the other hand, is perceived as a participation in natural process—a view from which Morris will begin to shift in the summer stories.

These themes are given a more extended treatment in "The Doom of King Acrisius," first of the April narratives. Warned that his daughter's son will slay him, the king of Argos imprisons Danaë in a brazen tower. Despite these precautions, Jove comes to her as a golden shower, and her son Perseus—after various accomplishments, including the rescue and marriage of Andromeda—kills Acrisius by accident while taking part in a set of games. The story's title is at odds with the limited appearances of Acrisius in the narrative, but it suggests a unifying theme missing in the episodic account of Perseus' adventures. Without Acrisius, the hero's acts are merely a formless response to circumstances. It is the character who attempts to shape his own destiny—albeit, mistakenly—to whom Morris looked for the aesthetic structure of the tale.

Of the remaining spring narratives, the two told by the Wanderers are simple fables of frustrated pride or avarice. "The Proud King" (April) recounts the legend of Jovinian, a ruler whose belief "that he was something more than man, if not equal to God" (III, 242) is shattered when he wakes to discover himself a naked man, no longer recognized as king. Sufficiently humbled, he is restored to his kingdom, and at the end of his life he records his experience as a lesson—ironically, unheeded—for future kings. In the second May story, "The Writing on the Image," a scholar learned in "strange lore" and "sorcery" interprets an ancient marker and discovers a series of underground chambers, where images of the dead sit at a feast table, bedecked and surrounded with treasure. He loads his sack with gold and jewels, but when he attempts to seize "a wonderful green stone," a mechanical archer shoots the great carbuncle whose light had illuminated the room. The scholar is left trapped in darkness while overhead a storm effaces the evidence of his descent. Despite its treatment of the theme of hubris, "The Proud King" is an anomaly in *The Earthly Paradise*. In no other tale is the moral lesson so clear-cut; the possibility of moral transformation so unambiguously handled. In contrast, the May story's description of living death in an underground treasure house introduces an image that will haunt Morris' imagination in subsequent tales.

The Elder's familiar "Story of Cupid and Psyche" synthesizes the thematic concerns of the spring group and prepares the reader for the following seasons. The story's pattern of union, separation, trial, and reunion will recur in some form in ten of the eighteen summer, fall, and winter narratives. For the first time in the series, love is explicitly a marriage of human and divine orders, and Psyche, unlike her prototypes—Danaë and Andromeda—achieves real immortality. Appropriately, Psyche's quest is the most difficult ordeal in the spring section. Three times she contemplates suicide, and her final task for Venus leads her to the depths of the underworld. Like the scholar in "The Writing on the Image," she is confronted with an opulent feast of the dead, but she rejects the temptation and is allowed to return to the surface of the earth. Even so, her final moments with Proserpine take her perilously near a vision of despair that foreshadows Morris' later treatments of the union-separation-reunion archetype.

It has been argued that Psyche's trials are a direct result of her "failure in patience and trust."[6] But surely "the pain and difficulty of her journey to redemption" is an inescapable prerequisite to immortality. Despite its comforts, her sojourn in Cupid's place is at best the half-life of untested innocence. Succumbing to the temptation of knowledge is a *felix culpa* that forces Psyche to pass through the world of fallen experience—as far as the despairing perception William Blake would have identified with Ulro—in order to achieve the organized vision of the immortals. Just as the Wanderers' quest was born out of their awareness of death, so, too, Psyche can only enter the state of eternal love after having confronted its opposite.

The summer stories reflect the increasing seriousness of Morris' thought and his growing skill as a storyteller. In "Atalanta's Race" the hero's victory was sufficient unto itself. In "The Love of Alcestis," first of the June tales, winning his bride is only half of Admetus' story. Condemned to labor for a mortal for the space of a year, Apollo attaches himself to the king of Pherae. With the god's aid, Admetus fulfills the demand that her bridegroom arrive in a chariot drawn by a lion and a wild boar and weds Alcestis, daughter of Pelias. His services completed, Apollo leaves with the promise to come to Admetus' aid when he is faced with death. Years pass, and Admetus on his deathbed summons the god, who grants him renewed life on the condition that someone will die in his place. Admetus cannot conceive of anyone's making the sacrifice, but, without betraying her intentions, Alcestis lays down her life for her husband.

Admetus is a more complex figure than anyone in the spring stories. Like that of the Wanderers, his quests, first for Alcestis and then for renewed life, are ambivalent gestures. He is an overreacher who admits that his vow to win Alcestis was made in a moment of headstrong pride and whose joy in fulfilling her father's conditions is as much a matter of his own glory as it is of his love for the woman he has come to marry. The serpent that coils around Alcestis when Admetus seeks to consummate their marriage is explained as Diana's retribution for being ignored in the sacrificial offerings. But it also suggests Admetus' own impetuous attempt to seize a woman whom he as yet conceives as a token of his prowess rather than an independent human being.[7] Thus, the final irony of the story echoes a problem central to the narrative as a whole. Despite his preternatural longevity and the success of his reign, it is not Admetus but Alcestis whose memory is honored by subsequent generations.

The companion June poem, "The Lady of the Land," links Admetus' quests for erotic fulfillment and immortality with the imagery of "The Writing on the Image." Exploring a ruined palace on a desolate Greek island, an Italian pirate stumbles upon underground rooms in a state of remarkable preservation and a woman of extraordinary and irresistable beauty. She explains that for the past four hundred years she has endured the punishment of Diana, to whom she was promised as a virgin by her father and whose vow she broke by trying to take a lover. In revenge, the goddess transformed her into a dragon, but granted her her normal shape one day each year and the ability to become fully human if a lover would kiss her in her animal form. He promises to save her, but when he returns the next day, the sight of her as a dragon frightens him into running away. Overwhelmed by the experience, he dies after three days of nightmare ravings.

For the first time in the stories, the hero fails to rescue the virgin. For the first time, too, the tragic implications of her state are fully realized. Brooding over "the hidden heaps of gold" in her underground lair, the Lady of the Land possesses both the wealth and timeless permanence so many other characters in these stories—most recently, Admetus—have longed for. But to what avail?

"The Son of Croesus" reiterates the theme of the folly of trying to escape fate, but its focus is not on Croesus, who hopes to save his son from the doom prophesied him, but on Adrastus, the unwitting slayer of his friend, who determines finally that the only way to avert the future is suicide. The second July story, "The Watching of the Falcon," is a further comment on "The Lady of the Land" and "Cupid and Psyche." "The case of this falcon was such," the "Argument" explains, "that whoso watched it without sleeping for seven days and seven nights, had his first wish granted him by a fay lady, that appeared to him thereon; and some wished one thing, and some another. But a certain king, who watched the falcon daily, would wish for nought but the love of that fay; which wish being accomplished, was afterwards his ruin" (IV, 161). His kingdom overwhelmed, the

72

once prosperous ruler is murdered in his sleep by traitors. Thus, for the first time in the sequence, eros is at odds with political fortune. But the story is not so much a parable of the dangers of supernatural liasons as an expression of the insatiable hunger of the imagination itself. The king undertakes the quest precisely because he has apparently all a man could desire:

> unless the fay could give
> For ever on the earth to live,
> Nought could he ask that he had not:
> For boundless riches had he got,
> Fair children and a faithful wife;
> And happily had passed his life,
> And all fulfilled of victory,
> Yet was he fain this thing to see.

(IV, 165)

His is Baudelaire's quest "Au fond de l'inconnu pour trouver du *nouveau!*" ("to the abyss of the unknown in search of something new")—an expression of the "full hearts still unsatisfied" Morris describes in the second stanza of "The Apology." Unlike "The Writing on the Image" or "The Proud King," with which it shares a terse, parabolic structure, "The Watching of the Falcon" eludes easy moralizing. The king's fate is a result of his erotic quest, but his subsequent ill fortune is not a punishment for guilt but an arbitrary unfolding of events with no perceptible relationship to his actions.

This arbitrariness is all the more striking when we place the story against its August counterpart, "Ogier the Dane." Morgan le Fay— one of the six fays who blessed Ogier at his birth—arranges for him to come into her hands at the end of his heroic life. After a period of initial uneasiness, he accepts her "charmed crown of gold," and they live together joyfully in the timeless world of Avallon. The central event of the story is Ogier's last foray into human affairs. Sent to aid France and renew his fame, he forgets Avallon and, after great acts of heroism, is about to marry the widowed French queen. But Morgan le Fay appears on his wedding morning and leads Ogier back to her realm.

In "The Hill of Venus" (February), Morris will explore the moral ambiguities of a state resembling Avallon. But in this earlier tale, Ogier's doubts—and our own—are silenced by the narrator's reassurances. Unlike the king in "The Watching of the Falcon," Ogier is able to enjoy the best of both worlds. If this is to be explained in terms of a difference between the figures, it may lie in Ogier's passivity. Entering Avallon through a series of dreams, Ogier offers a strong contrast to the king's seven-day abstinence from sleep. Like Psyche, the other spring-summer figure who effects a permanent liason with a supernatural being, he is drawn into the relationship solely through the agency of his lover. But unlike Psyche, Ogier is never confronted with the need to exert himself to recover his lost love. And so, despite the official tally of his heroics, Ogier pales beside the endurance of Psyche and the suffering of the watcher king.

Yet neither Psyche nor the king is the central embodiment of the erotic quester in the 1868 volume. This honor goes to the hero of "Pygmalion and the Image," the penultimate summer story, who—by no accident—is an artist. The process through which his statue is transformed into a living woman is the highpoint of imaginative and erotic fulfillment in the *Earthly Paradise* stories. Commencing his work, Pygmalion prays to Venus, who "well content, / Unto his hand such godlike mastery sent, / That like the first artificer he wrought/Who made the gift that woe to all men brought" (IV, 190). Pygmalion's art is "godlike" because it is the unrepressed expression of his own libido. Creating the statue is thus a gesture of erotic self-discovery, in which art ceases to be an evasion of "thought's poisonous sting" (IV, 190) and confronts him directly with the object of his own desire. (It is thus comparable to the art of *The Earthly Paradise* itself, insofar as Morris uses the poem as a medium through which to clarify the nature of his own libido.) But this "godlike mastery" is two-edged. The work by its very nature is the agent of his fall from a state equivalent to Eden. The completed artifact is like Eve because differentiating himself from the object of desire tempts Pygmalion from the comfortable solipsism of his earlier life.

Pygmalion's statue is a Pre-Raphaelite figure that could be one of Rossetti's paintings of Jane Morris:

> with one hand
> Reached out, as to a lover, did it stand,
>
> The other held a fair rose over-blown;
> No smile was on the parted lips, the eyes
> Seemed as if even now great love had shown
> Unto them, something of its sweet surprise,

Yet saddened them with half-seen mysteries,
And still midst passion maiden-like she seemed;
As though of love unchanged for aye, she dreamed.

(IV, 194)

But it is not Pygmalion's skill as an artist that constitutes the primary interest of the story. Rather, it is the problematic nature of his relationship to his finished work. Pygmalion's liberated imagination creates an image of desire that threatens to overwhelm his identity. Never a man fully integrated with society, he is menaced with total alienation by the presence of the statue. His emotional pangs do not simply reflect his separation from the object of his desire, but derive from his awareness of the impossibility of realizing the ideal his imagination has revealed to him.

Significantly, the statue's metamorphosis can only occur after Pygmalion has come to terms with the dangerous prevalence of his imagination. He must reach the state of mind in which he loathes "to see the image fair,/White and unchanged of face," and when, "as a man awakening from a dream,"

nought seemed good
In all the things that he before had deemed
At least worth life, and on his heart there streamed
Cold light of day—

(IV, 202)

Then, and only then, is his prayer to Venus answered, his passion consumated with a real woman.

Pygmalion's erotic quest is thus another analogue to that of the Wanderers, and at the same time it offers an ironic counterpart to Morris' own marriage with a Pre-Raphaelite beauty who turned from a living woman into a statue. As a development of the union-separation-reunion archetype, "Pygmalion and the Image" also clarifies the significance of the separation stage. The higher marriage of poet-lover with the object of his imaginative desire is only possible through that double recognition of the barrenness of nature and the inadequacy of the imagination toward which *The Earthly Paradise* will move rapidly in its final sections.

IV   The Earthly Paradise: *Fall and Winter*

Morris' summer vision culminates in "Ogier the Dane," in which erotic fulfillment effectively separates the hero from the world of living men. From Ogier's dreamy isolation it is a small step to the recognition that erotic fulfillment is a potentially alienating experience. "The Death of Paris," first of the September stories, marks this transition. Wounded by Philoctetes' arrow, Paris is borne from Troy to Mt. Ida in search of the nymph Œnone, whom he had once loved and who alone can heal him. They meet and speak. She is tempted to save him, despite his perfidy; he, to speak loving words to her, half in truth, half in an effort to save himself. But she eventually turns away, having determined that Paris' present death is preferable to the death he would unavoidably have met had he returned to Troy. And he dies, "with a mighty cry/Of 'Helen, Helen, Helen!'"

For the first time in *The Earthly Paradise* Morris presents a genuinely tragic situation, and for the first time he is able to satisfactorily handle the figure of a betrayed lover who acts out her feelings with strength and dignity. "The Death of Paris" is tragic because both characters have valid, but mutually unresolvable needs. Right and wrong, good and evil are no longer applicable categories of judgment, as they were in the moral fables of spring and summer. For once, the hero is forced to choose between two legitimate ideals—pastoral and heroic love. He wavers. But his ultimate cry to Helen affirms the necessity of choice. Like Ogier, Paris approaches Œnone's world through a series of dreams and awakenings. But unlike Morgan le Fay she is not prepared to take back the lover who has deserted her in preference for the heroic world. And so he dies, far from the scene of battle with neither Œnone nor Helen at his side—a man whose quest for love and honor has brought him only an intensified awareness of his own isolation.

Among the finest pieces in *The Earthly Paradise,* the second September story, "The Land East of the Sun and West of the Moon" returns us to the trancelike fairy-tale world of "Ogier the Dane." However, the terms of the plot are reversed. John, youngest of three Norwegian brothers, sets out to watch his father's meadow, the grass of which has been mysteriously trodden down the previous three nights. Seven swan maidens appear, undress, and dance. He falls in love with their leader and secures her skin; when the others reclothe themselves and fly away, she is left behind. After a difficult confrontation, she responds to his passion and transports him—through a dream—to an otherworldly land where they live in bliss. Three years pass. He breaks the spell by wondering about his home and family, and she responds by telling him he must go back to Norway and abide a sign from her, to which she adds the warning that disaster will occur if he speaks aloud of his longing for her. John's trial of patience is structurally akin to Psyche's, but while she is moved to break her vow on the relatively flimsy grounds of fear and curiosity, John breaks his out of uncontrollable passion—complicated by his need to explain himself to the sister-in-law who has thrown herself at his feet. The swan-maiden appears and spends one night with him in his father's house, but before dawn she leaves him, hoping in despair that her words will somehow penetrate to his dreaming consciousness: "My feet, lost Love, shall wander soon/*East of the Sun, West of the Moon!*" (V, 82).

Waking to his loss, John sets forth on the search that will occupy the chief years of his life and see him grow into middle age. Finally, shipwrecked on the Indian ocean, he is washed ashore somewhere in the southern hemisphere, where he finds his love, together with the people of her pastoral kingdom, living in a state of suspended consciousness. He awakens her to full life, the land and its inhabitants are reborn, and they live together in happiness.

However, a mere synopsis of the fairy tale cannot suggest the rich complexity of Morris' retelling. Its most remarkable characteristic is the fable of poetic creativity in its narrative frame. Gregory the Star-gazer is sent as skipper of a fishing mission for the Norwegian court. The story is his dream, interrupted and finally concluded by three wakenings during the course of the night and early morning. In the introductory section, he dreams of an unidentified "gold-clad man" who enters King Magus' Christmastide celebrations and offers the tale as repayment for the king's hospitality. But as the story commences, "That strange man in the royal weed/Grew" to Gregory "his other self" (V, 27). In the first interruption—immediately following the union of John and the swan-maiden—this identification is complete; in the second—after she has left John sleeping in his father's house—

> the King's hall and feast did pass
> Clean from his mind; and now it seemed
> That of no tale-telling he dreamed,
> But of his own life grown to be
> A new and marvellous history.

(V, 85)

But in the third and final wakening, "O'er Gregory's eyes the pain of morn/Flashed suddenly" (V, 119), and the identification abruptly terminates. Instead, "the bright/Broad day" faces him with an acute awareness of loss and a sense of alienation from his fellows. At length, he painfully readjusts himself to reality and writes out his dream as the poem, "The Land East of the Sun and West of the Moon." In "Pygmalion and the Image," creation of a physical artifact is the first stage in realizing the full potential of the imagination. Reversing this sequence, Gregory's poem illustrates Shelley's observation that "the most glorious poetry that has ever been communicated to the world is probably a feeble shadow of the original conception of the Poet."[8] Like the Wanderers' own stories, it is at once an attempt to sustain the "fading coal" of vision and an anodyne to the pain of waking from vision to "the light of common day."

Gregory and John are versions of the same character. The "slothful" son, "wont in summer heats to go/About the garden to and fro,/Plucking the flowers . . . and muttering . . . Old rhymes that few men understood" (V, 27), and the "Star-gazer" are both men of the imagination who pay for their intense inner life with estrangement from their fellow human beings. Morris' poem is thus a study of the relationship between a poet and his literary projection. It begins with Gregory's identification with the "gold-clad" storyteller—an heroic analogue to the "wizard" in "The Apology." Through this idealization of his own role, Gregory is able to make the subsequent identification with John himself. However, this occurs when John's fortunes are at their lowest, and John's reunion with his bride causes Gregory's waking to "the bright/Broad day." His projection as the central figure of his romance is incomplete wish-fulfillment. Significantly, the story focuses on the pain of separation and the agony of John's all but hopeless quest. Although the tale ends in assurances of the lovers' "bliss," its closing phrase acknowledges "That love can ne'er be satisfied." Hopeless desire—whether the lover's for his beloved or the poet's for self-fulfillment in his own work—is the theme of the story.

And this theme repeats itself—with a twist—in the only one of the October tales that need concern us, "The Man Who Never Laughed Again." (The Elder's "Story of Acontius and Cydippe" is still another version of the virgin-rescued-from-Diana theme—strangely out of place in the fall volume—and Morris confessed himself "not sanguine about it.") Having fallen from high estate, Bharam is taken up by a former companion and installed as the guardian of a company of "doleful men" who dwell in a palace of great opulence, grimly awaiting death. In return for his services, Bharam is promised the contents of the palace when the last of the men has died. They refuse to explain the cause of their misery, but warn him away from a mysterious door in the side of a cliff. His task completed, Bharam naturally breaks the prohibition and enters the door. He falls into a swoon and wakens to find himself being brought to wed the beautiful queen of a wealthy kingdom. After two years, she announces she must depart for one hundred days and leaves him with the injunction not to enter "the room where thou and I/Were left alone that day of all sweet days" (V, 195). He restrains himself, but at last succumbs to curiosity. Inside the room he finds a cup with an inscription enjoining him to " 'Drink . . . and be rememberèd/When all are gone whose feet the green earth touch' ":

> "be bold,
> And things unthought of shall thine eyes behold!
>
> "Yea, thou must drink, for if thou drinkest not
> Nor soundest all the depths of this hid thing,
> Think'st thou that these my words can be forgot,
> How close soever thou to love mayst cling,
> How much soever thou art still a king?"
>
> (V, 200)

He drinks, collapses, and wakens back before the door in the cliff, now shut to him forever—and thus begins his life as "the man who never laughed again."

A revision of the union-separation-reunion paradigm, Bharam's story reverses the happy ending of the earlier versions and leaves us with a man eternally tormented by his inability to sustain the erotic intensity he briefly experienced. Psyche breaks Cupid's prohibition on account of her vulnerable innocence; John breaks the swan-maiden's because of the unbearable strength of his passion; Bharam succumbs to the nagging hunger of the imagination itself. His act is motivated by the same inescapable need to penetrate to deeper levels of experience that led him to enter the forbidden door in the first place. Thus, only a man with Bharam's particular sensibility could have attained the bliss he realizes, but that same sensibility renders him incapable of sustaining it for any length of time. And the possibility that his two years of happiness may simply have been a dream enforces our sense of the liabilities of imaginative fulfillment.

The darkened tenor of the autumn group is evident in the first of the November tales, "The Story of Rhodope." Its Cinderella fable of a girl elevated from humble surroundings to become the wife of a great king would not have been out of place among the earlier stories. But Morris chooses to focus on the alienation from family and countrymen that derives from Rhodope's awareness of herself as a special person. Separated from the father whose love has been her one emotional satisfaction, it is not with joy but stoicism that she accepts the new role in which she finds herself at the conclusion of the story.

Longest of the *Earthly Paradise* narratives, "The Lovers of Gudrun" is among the first fruits of Morris' study of Icelandic (which we shall take up more fully in the next chapter). The story is based on the Laxdale Saga, and treats the love triangle of Gudrun and the foster-brothers Bodli and Kiartin. From childhood, both men are in love with Gudrun. The heroic Kiartin, to whom—after two short-lived early marriages—she plights herself, leaves Iceland to win fame at the court of the Norwegian king, Olaf Tryggvison. Bodli journeys with him, but returns first, along with the rumor that Kiartin is wooing Tryggvison's sister. Believing herself betrayed, Gudrun marries Bodli. But Kiartin returns, thus alienating Gudrun from Bodli and establishing the grounds for a feud between his and their family. Prompted by Gudrun's brothers, the feud grows increasingly bitter. Kiartin marries, thus further estranging himself from Gudrun. At last, to avenge themselves for Kiartin's theft of their livestock, her brothers force Bodli to join them in an ambush on his foster-brother. Kiartin allows himself to be killed in single combat with Bodli. After the death of his foster-father, who has held off his other sons from revenging themselves for Kiartin's death, Bodli too is killed. Gudrun eventually marries once again, but outlives her last husband as she has all the others.

The strength of the poem lies in its slow but inexorable unfolding of events—the deterioration of the once powerful bond between the two families, the undermining of Bodli's efforts to prevent the breach, the metamorphosis of Gudrun's love for Kiartin into a self-destructive commitment to revenge. Morris has been criticized for softening the bare-facts objectivity of his source. But "The Lovers of Gudrun" is a successful poem largely because of the psychological empathy Morris brings to bear on its characters. In developing the narrative, Morris shifts its concentration from Gudrun—"the Icelandic Helen"—to Bodli, torn between his deep love for the man he has, in the weakness of his own passion, betrayed and his loyalty to the family of Gudrun, whose real feelings toward him he is never able to know. Returning from the ambush of Kiartin, he confronts her with the deed he has accomplished at her behest against the strongest promptings of his own conscience:

> She reached a hand
> Out towards the place where trembling he did stand
> But touched him not, and never did he know
> If she had mind some pity then to show
> Unto him, or if rather more apart
> She fain had thrust him from her raging heart.

(V, 383)

The abyss between husband and wife is not the failure of passion, but the final triumph of selfhood over understanding.

In contrast with the intensely felt tales of autumn, certain of the Winter stories manifest a newfound detachment from the thematic concerns of the poem. This is particularly true for the three classical stories—"The Golden Apples" (December), "Bellerophon at Argos" (January), and "Bellerophon in Lycia" (February). The first of this group retells the simple tale of Hercules' quest for the golden apples of the Hesperides. By shattering the door to their Garden so that "into the guarded place bright poured the day" (VI, 10), Hercules effects a synthesis of the imagination-nature dualism that runs throughout *The Earthly Paradise*. Yet by presenting the hero's actions through the eyes of the Phoenician merchants whose vessel he has commandeered for the expedition, Morris emphasizes the special nature of the man capable of this radical gesture. Moreover, Hercules himself is subject to fate, and the poem is no more than a passing episode in a drama that exceeds human comprehension.

The two Bellerophon stories develop this new image of the hero. In the first, Hipponoüs, son of the king of Corinth, comes to Argos after "unwittingly" slaying his brother. He is received by Proetus, purged of guilt, and renamed Bellerophon. But Proetus' wife Sthenobœa falls in love with Bellerophon, whom, having been repulsed, she accuses of attempting to rape her. He is sent to Proetus' father-in-law Jobates, king of Lycia, bearing Proetus' request that he be put to death. Sthenobœa commits suicide. In the second story, Jobates attempts to carry out Proetus' instructions, compelled against his will by his debt to the man who once saved his life. He sends Bellerophon on a series of desperate missions: he quells the rebellion of a barbarous subject people; he overcomes a force of Amazons who are laying waste to the countryside; he slays the Chimera, for which he is rewarded with the hand of Jobates' remaining daughter, Philonoë. Finally, when his outright attempt to assassinate Bellerophon is foiled, Jobates shows the hero Proetus' letter, the two men are reconciled, and Bellerophon is elevated to the throne of Lycia.

Bellerophon is the counterpart to the spring group's Perseus. But unlike Perseus he is not only a slayer of monsters, but a self-scrutinizing human being. Morris is less concerned with his actions than with his introspection, and as a result his physical heroism assumes a secondary role in the story. Moreover, in the first of the two narratives devoted to the events in his life Morris seems more interested in Sthenobœa, the victim of not unreasonable passion, than Bellerophon. And in the second, Bellerophon's heroism is presented to the reader through various intermediaries—never directly by the narrator himself. For example, we learn the details of Bellerophon's slaying the Chimera—one of the minor triumphs of *The Earthly Paradise*—through a young man-at-arms lucky enough to have survived his own attempt at the monster. (Similarly, Sthenobœa's tragic death is narrated by a fisherman, who happened to witness it and tells the story to his wife.) Seen from the perspective of Morris' later thought, this shift from the glorification of the hero suggests his growing awareness of the larger context of heroic action. And yet it also expresses Morris' recognition of the fundamental isolation of the hero. Indeed, Bellerophon, who begins his tale as a fratricide and whose life is a series of rejections by father figures, suggests an effort to assimilate the classical hero with the romantic tradition of the poet-outcast.

In the spring and summer stories, events define character; in fall, characters are the victims of events; in winter, there is a fundamental absurdity in the relationship between a character and the events he undergoes. Hence, the classical legends, with their equation of deeds and character, become more and more alien to Morris' vision, and—despite his attempt to redefine classical heroism—the three winter stories told by the Wanderers appear to be closer to his heart.

"The Fostering of Aslaug" (December) is another recasting of Icelandic saga. Aslaug, the daughter of Sigurd and Byrnhild, is rescued from the social upheaval surrounding the deaths of her parents by the craftsman Heimir, who takes to the road disguised as a minstrel. Heimir is murdered by peasants, and the girl, whom he had hidden within the base of his harp, is rediscovered and raised as their child. Again, Morris employs a Cinderella fable, in which Aslaug is eventually saved from her brutal surroundings and wed to a king.

Unlike Rhodope's her marriage entails more than a stoic acceptance
of fate. Nevertheless, the story's focus on the peasant couple stresses
a level of human meanness absent from the earlier narratives, and the
shadow of her parents' tragedy darkens the events of the heroine's
story.

Paired with the two Bellerophon tales, the January and February
narratives center in the medievalized Venus—transformed from the
goddess of love into a demon-temptress. In this transformation
Morris may have been influenced by Swinburne, whose "Laus
Veneris" and "Dolores," published in 1866, had treated a similar
archetype of the *femme fatale*—although Morris was later to observe
that he had never been able to "really sympathize with Swinburne's
work" *(Letters,* 158) and Rossetti, whose poetry he did admire, dealt
with analogous figures. In "The Ring Given to Venus" the newlywed
Laurence places his ring mockingly on the finger of a statue of the
goddess. When he returns to regain it, her fingers are closed; when
he returns with a file and chisel, the ring is gone altogether. Each
time he attempts to consummate his marriage he falls into a swoon
and finds himself in the arms of the goddess, on whose finger he
recognizes his ring. (Thus it is no longer Diana who prevents erotic
fulfillment, as in the spring and summer stories; but rather it is the
goddess of love herself who blocks the hero's socialized marriage.)

Laurence's father-in-law takes him to Palumbus, a Faustian monk
who—at the cost of his own soul—instructs him as to how he may
regain the ring. Waiting through the night on an eroding promontory
by the sea, he is confronted by a procession of the pagan gods in their
debased state. He addresses himself to Jupiter and, presenting him
with Palumbus' scroll, is granted his request. At dawn the voice of
Venus comes to him from a cloud—

> "Thou who has wrought me added shame,
> Take back thine own and go thy ways;
> And think, perchance, in coming days,
> When all grows old about thee, how
> From foolish hands thou needs must throw
> A gift of unhoped great delight."

(VI, 172)

Finding his spousal ring on the grass at his feet, Laurence returns
"full of joy" to town.

> As for Palumbus, tossed about
> His soul might be in dread and doubt,
> In rest at least his body lay
> Ere the great bell struck noon that day.
>
> (VI, 173)

Seen against the prophecy of Venus and the death of his ambiguous benefactor, Laurence's regaining of his ring is a small success in a small world, and we are more touched by the losers in the tale than by its jejune protagonist. Within the terms of the story, Venus represents a primitive eroticism suppressed by Christianity that threatens Laurence's "normal" sexual life. Instead of coming to terms with this eroticism, he merely rejects it. Hence, it is difficult to accept the conclusion of the story as a genuine resolution of his problem.

Yet the alternative to Laurence Morris offers in the final story is hardly an easy solution to the problem of integrating pagan energy with Christian self-consciousness. Morris' retelling of the Tannhäuser legend is among the crucial narratives in *The Earthly Paradise*. Driven by "longings nought could satisfy," Walter enters the cavern that leads to Venus' underground paradise. Becoming her paramour, he grows "exceeding wise in love." But in time

> a great longing would there stir in him
> That all these kisses might not satisfy;
> Dreams never dreamed before would gather dim
> About his eyes, and trembling would he cry
> To tell him how it was he should not die;
> To tell him how it was that he alone
> Should have a love all perfect and his own.
>
> (VI, 297)

Venus—like Gudrun—will not answer his questions. At length, his doubt drives him from her. He reenters the world, but finds himself as estranged from the "cold day" of reality as he had been tortured by the goddess' silences. He joins a band of pilgrims journeying to Rome, where he is granted an interview with the pope. The confrontation between these two men—the pope, torn between his human response to Walter and his sense of the special role he must sustain, and Walter, longing to unburden his conscience but unable to disavow the love he feels with renewed strength—sharpens the conflict between socializing Christianity and pagan individualism.

Walter announces his intention to return to the Hill of Venus, and "a stern look came o'er" the "kind vexed face" of the pope: " 'Yea dwell there evermore!'/He cried: 'just so much hope I have of thee/As on this dry staff fruit and flowers to see!' " (VI, 323). Walter flees back to the arms of Venus—to "sleepless nights of horrors passing hell" and "joys by which our joys are misery;/But hopeless both" (VI, 323). The pope, alone in his garden, ponders his parting words to Walter:

> "Oh God, if I have done Thee deadly wrong,
> And lost a soul Thou wouldst have saved and blessed,
> Yet other words Thou knowest were on my tongue,
> When 'twixt that word and mine Thine image pressed:
> Thou wilt remember this and give him rest!"
>
> (VI, 325)

He stoops to raise his staff and finds it sending forth leaves, "wondrous flowers," and fruit. "Too glad for smiles, or fears, or any speech," he dies in the joy of the miracle.

Walter is *The Earthly Paradise*'s ultimate erotic quester. He rejects the women of the real world because "Words of old stories, turned to images/Of lovelier things would blur the sight of them." Responding to the beauty of the sunset, "mid the full sweetness of the spring," the pope wishes "That man and I this peace together trod!" (VI, 324). But it is precisely the beauty of the natural world that Walter has found inadequate to his imagination. On the other hand, Walter is fully aware that the alternative of Venus' "sunless" realm is itself at best a "lovely dream" (VI, 299). Ironically, he can never learn of the miracle that confirms his salvation. But it is the essence of Walter's choice that he cannot foresee its outcome. Thus the closing episode vindicates his quest precisely insofar as it reaffirms the moral ambiguity of his actions.

As Morris' final statement of the union-separation-reunion archetype, "The Hill of Venus" takes us one step beyond the resigned aestheticism of "The Land East of the Sun and West of the Moon." The energy frustrated by Gregory's inability to achieve the otherworldly marriage of his dream is sublimated into the writing of a poem. But Walter is insusceptible to the anodyne of creativity. His return to Venus is thus not a rejection of romantic love—although it is certainly a severe comment on it—but a rejection of escapist poetry, all the stronger a gesture for the role that poetry played in sending him to Venus in the first place. Reentering the Hill of Venus is thus equivalent to giving up the enterprise of *The Earthly Paradise* itself—or, more generally speaking, to giving up the kind of narrative poetry that characterizes *The Earthly Paradise*.

The final volume of *The Earthly Paradise* marked the end of the first major stage in Morris' development. Despite the poem's popular reception, Morris did not continue writing narrative poetry in the style his newfound audience so greatly admired. Yet, seen either as a purely poetic expression or as an exercise in psychological self-discovery, *The Earthly Paradise* was at least a partial success. Indeed, its major sections—"The Wanderers," "Cupid and Psyche," "The Land East of the Sun and West of the Moon," "The Lovers of Gudrun," "The Hill of Venus"—are among the most important (and least fully appreciated) narrative poems of the nineteenth century. Significant documents in the history of late romanticism, they guarantee Morris' status as a major narrative poet in the English language.

CHAPTER 4

"The Great Story of the North": Iceland, Love is Enough, *and* The Story of Sigurd the Volsung

IF Rossetti, the son of an Italian expatriot and the translator of Dante, was an exemplar of Mediterranean culture, it is understandable that Morris' rejection of Rossetti entailed a turn from the geography and literature of the South to those of the North. But his journeys to Iceland and translations of the sagas were not merely a reaction against Rossetti; they were a positive attempt to rediscover the Germanic roots of Anglo-Saxon civilization. Like *The Earthly Paradise*, his recreations of the literature of the North were acts of personal self-discovery. But unlike the earlier poem, they were also explicit acts of cultural self-discovery. In them, Morris no longer speaks as an isolated individual; rather, he expresses the fundamental connection between his own fate and that of his society. And it is in this respect that the 1870s effected the transition from the qualified aestheticism of the 1860s[1]—the period of Rossetti's greatest influence on his work—to the social activitism of Morris' final decades.

I Icelandic Journals *(1871, 1873)*

Morris' Icelandic experience corresponds to the crises pivotal in the development of many Victorian intellectuals.[2] But unlike the typical "crisis" autobiography—Tennyson's *In Memoriam*, the central chapters of Carlyle's *Sartor Resartus* and Mill's *Autobiography*—Morris' *Icelandic Journals* replace direct self-analysis with a comparatively objective account of his two expeditions to Iceland. He revised the 1871 journal in the spring of 1873—a precondition for the return trip he was planning that summer—but he never published it and left the manuscript with Georgiana Burne-Jones. The fragmentary 1873 "diary" is unrevised, its final entries little more than jottings. Hence, it is the former with which we shall be chiefly concerned.

The dominant mood of the 1871 journey is innocence. Morris is a young bachelor once more, seeing the world with fresh eyes. And there is a complementary boyishness in his carryings on. Exploring the Faroes, Morris and his companions "drank unlimited milk, and then turned back up the slopes, but lay down a little way off the house, and ate and drank, thoroughly comfortable, and enjoying the rolling about in the fresh grass prodigiously" (VIII, 16). "Horseplay," spasms of "inextinguishable laughter," and frank quarreling characterize the interplay between the travelers. Morris writes about himself with a keen sense of self-parody, creating an autobiographical persona that exorcises his insecurity by reducing it to comic triviality. He dramatizes his "cockney" ineptitude, which precipitates, among other things, a memorable "series of losses"—first of his tin pannikin, then of one of his slippers, later of the haversack containing his journal and spare pipe, and, near the end of the expedition, of the oars to a boat he was supposed to have been rowing. On the other hand, the journal balances his clumsiness in riding and climbing—because, as an Icelandic priest frankly explained, "you know you are so fat"—with his success in confecting a series of well-made stews under the most difficult of circumstances.

But his journey is more than a pilgrimage to the "land of the sagas" and more than a return to schoolboy innocence. It is also an act of putting himself, literally, in a world defined by its narrative art. The artistic dimension to Morris' quest is explicit in the first journal entries. The countryside after York is "dull and undramatic" (VIII, 2), but as the train takes him further north, "the country gets cleaner" and at last, with the sight of Holy Island and the North Sea, "poetical-looking" (VIII, 2). The valleys of Scotland, which he was seeing for the first time, have "a wonderfully poetical character about them . . . rather like one's imagination of what the backgrounds to the border ballads ought to be" (VIII, 3). Edinburgh "must have been an impressive and poetical place," but is now "very doleful" because "the poetry is pretty much gone" (VIII, 3). This concern intensifies when Morris reaches the Faroes, his "first sight of a really northern land," whose "wild strange hills and narrow sounds . . . had something, I don't know what, of poetic and attractive about them" (VIII, 12). Viewed from a mountain ridge, the islands' central firth seemed "like nothing I had ever seen, but strangely like my old imaginations of places for sea-wanderers to come to" (VIII, 14). The landscape touches him with "the air of romanticism," and an isolated farm strikes him as "a most beautiful and poetical place" (VIII, 15).

But the "poetry" of the Faroes is qualified by another, equally significant response. His "first sight of a really northern land" confronts Morris with a nature "not savage but mournfully empty and barren" (VIII, 11). And having called Kirkiubœ farm "a most beautiful and poetical place," he goes on to acknowledge it "more remote and melancholy than I can say, in spite of the flowers and grass and bright sun: it looked as if you might live for a hundred years before you would ever see ship sailing into the bay there; as if the old life of the saga-time had gone, and the modern life never reached the place" (VIII, 15). Thus the relationship between northern landscape and its poetic past is essentially elegiac: Morris' search for a world in which timeless nature is infused with a timeless human imagination confronts him with a barren landscape, where Kirkiubœ farm stands—as Matthew Arnold described himself in "Stanzas from the Grande Chartreuse"—"between two worlds, one dead, the other powerless to be born."

Morris' attunement to Kelmscott's "melancholy" involved a comparable sense of isolation in historical time and natural setting. His confrontation with the North was needed to organize these feelings into a general attitude toward human experience. However, he appears to have known what he was looking for. Thus, his response to the Faroes typifies his response to the North as a whole. Expectations of "poetic" beauty give way to a recognition of the profoundly alien nature of the landscape, which in turn gives way to a new, more chastened sense of the sublime. Morris' account of leaving the Faroes illustrates this pattern:

I turned to look ahead as the ship met the first of the swell in the open sea, and when I looked astern a very few minutes after, I could see nothing at all of the gates we had come out by, no slopes of grass, or valleys opening out from the shore; nothing but a terrible wall of rent and furrowed rocks, the little clouds still entangled here and there about the tops of them: here the wall would be rent from top to bottom and its two sides would yawn as if they would have fallen asunder, here it was buttressed with great masses of stone that had slipped from its top; there it ran up into all manner of causeless-looking spikes: there was no beach below the wall, no foam breaking at its feet. It was midnight now and everything was grey and colourless and shadowless, yet there was light enough in the clear air to see every cranny and nook of the rocks, and in the north-east now the grey sky began to get a little lighter with dawn. I stood near the stern and looked backward a long time till the coast, which had seemed a great crescent when we came out of the sound, was now a long flat line, and so then I went to bed, with the sky brightening quickly. (VIII, 17–18)

Morris turns to renew his pleasure in the embracing openness of the natural world, only to discover the gate closed, no longer even recognizable as a gate, and the hospitable landscape transformed into an image of "causeless" material force precipitating "grey and colourless" ruin. But this "midnight" vision yields on closer scrutiny first to an almost preternatural clarity and then to the light of dawn itself. The perception that nature is empty and fundamentally inhuman enables Morris to respond with detached, chastened pleasure to a beauty characterized by brightness without warmth.

Morris' experience of the Faroes is echoed in his day-by-day account of the Icelandic terrain, in which beauty is inseparable from desolation. The adjectives that recur in his descriptions are "desolate," "gloomy," "ugly," "melancholy," "dismal," "awful," "dreadful," and "horrible." Not infrequently he is "a little downhearted with the savagery of the place." But this "heart-sickness" can give way to profounder feelings. The central episode of the 1871 journey is Morris' crossing the desolate interior "wilderness" (VIII, 75–89). Not merely defined by the absence of human habitations, the wilderness is a place in its own right. It has a "wall" and a "gate" (like the Faroe islands) that "impresses itself on my memory as a peculiarly solemn place" (VIII, 75) and, once passed, "shuts us out from the rest of the world on that side." The "Waste of Long-Jokul . . . looks as if it ended the world, green-white and gleaming in the doubtful sun" (VIII, 76). This is Morris' zero vision—his personal realization of the imagery of "The Apology" to *The Earthly Paradise:* a terminal world in which even the light—like the warmth—of the sun is "doubtful." And appropriately it is here, in the most physically trying section of the expedition, that Morris has "the most horrible sight of mountains . . . the whole journey long" (VIII, 77). But the passage of this "dreadful waste" is a turning point in Morris' journal. Struggling against a stiff wind and a 1 August snowstorm, Morris pauses to drink at a stream and "felt a thrill of pride as a traveller, and a strange sensation, as I noted and cried out that it was running north." "About here, when all the others were getting to their worst, I began to revive, which I am glad of, for I got an impression of a very wonderful country" (VIII, 87–88). He has been morose and homesick, sunken in "dreaming of people at home," half-asleep on his pony. But one kind of withdrawal gives way to another. His spirits rise at the very time the rest of the party's have begun to fail. This sense of a separate self and his exhilarated response to the "wonderful country" are mutually sustaining elements of Morris' reflex from depression. Precisely because he is acutely aware of his separation from nature, he is able to look on it with renewed gusto. Precisely because of his gusto, his self-confidence is restored.

Two other passages, in which natural description gives way to introspection, confirm the importance of this pattern. The first is Morris' account of Thorsmark (VIII, 54). Again his response is twofold. The landscape is "closed" and "noiseless." Its waterfalls "seemed to go nowhere." He is not merely "cowed" by these negations. He is afraid he may be trapped in the hellish valley with its "brimstone-laden" river. Again, a gate shuts, but this time he is left (imaginatively) inside. Yet having submitted to this fear, he is then able to experience the second phase of his response: "a feeling of exaltation" and a corollary awareness of the human imagination's ability to "kindle amid such scenes"—an image structurally comparable to the sunlight's brightening the "grey and colourless" rocks of the Faroes coastline.

Morris' account of his visit to Laxdale is all the more significant on account of the specific associations of the landscape with his "Lovers of Gudrun." Characteristically, he withdraws from his companions, who busy themselves pitching the tent:

I spent my time alone in trying to regain my spirits which had suddenly fallen very low almost ever since we came into Laxdale.

Just think, though, what a mournful place this is—Iceland, I mean—setting aside the pleasure of one's animal life there: the fresh air, the riding and rough life, and feeling of adventure—how every place and name marks the death of its short-lived eagerness and glory; and withal so little is the life changed in some ways. . . . But Lord! what littleness and helplessness has taken the place of the old passion and violence that had place here once—and all is unforgotten; so that one has no power to pass it by unnoticed: yet that must be something of a reward for the old life of the land, and I don't think their life now is more unworthy than most people's elsewhere, and they are happy enough by seeming. Yet it is an awful place: set aside the hope that the unseen sea gives you here, and the strange threatening change of the blue spiky mountains beyond the firth, and the rest seems emptiness and nothing else: a piece of turf under your feet, and the sky overhead, that's all; whatever solace your life is to have here must come out of yourself or these old stories, not over hopeful themselves. Something of all this I thought; and besides our heads were now fairly turned homeward, and now and again a few times I felt homesick—I hope I may be forgiven. (VIII, 108)

The vacillation of the passage suggests a mind coming to terms with a difficult reality. Morris has "gone out for to see" a world in which landscape and legend are interfused; he discovers instead that legend is a crude, often ineffectual means of staving off the terrors of landscape. The journey may have been initiated in hopes of finding a synthesis missing in *The Earthly Paradise,* but the experience simply confirmed the lesson of the earlier poem. Seen as an alternative to the introspective despondency of the late 1860s, the "land of the sagas" may have tempted Morris with the possibility of violent, heroic action, but what he confronted instead was the smallness of human life and the emptiness of nature.

However, within the journals it is pure description more often than reflection that bears the burden of Morris' state of mind. The awareness of human fate he verbalizes at Laxdale can also express itself in the subdued manner and distance of his factual accounts of the landscape:

the mountains we look back on, toothed and jagged in an indescribable but well-remembered manner, are very noble and solemn. As we rode along the winding path here we saw a strange sight: a huge eagle quite within gunshot of us, and not caring at all for that, flew across and across our path, always followed by a raven that seemed teazing and buffeting him: this was the first eagle I had ever seen free and on the wing, and it was a glorious sight, no less; the curves of his flight, as he swept close by us, with every pen of his wings clear against the sky was something not to be forgotten. Out at sea too we saw a brigantine pitching about in what I thought must be a rough sea enough. The day has been much like yesterday throughout, and is getting clearer as it wears. (VIII, 119)

Once again Morris has passed a natural barrier—the mountains with their anthropomorphic "teeth"—rendered "noble and solemn" by distance. And his reward is the "free" flight of the eagle, which becomes, in a special sense, an expression of Morris' own freedom of perception. The experience is "something not to be forgotten," but Morris sets it down with Parnassian control. The eagle's curving flight echoes his own "winding path"; its movement on air, the liberation of the poet's consciousness able to shape his response to "teazing and buffeting" into aesthetic form; its isolation, his newfound sureness of individual identity. But Morris is able to record this "glorious sight" without forgetting that it is the expression of another order than his own. The very intensity of his vision derives from its precision and clarity—elements that depend on the detached equilibrium of the observer. This stark clarity of perception is Morris' lesson from Iceland. He participates in the eagle's flight, "every pen of his wings clear against the sky," without humanizing the eagle. He offers, without forcing, the implicit allegory of the raven's "teazing." He includes the expressive detail of the brigantine without apparent concern for the fate of its crew in the heavy seas. Unlike the ambiguous setting of *The Earthly Paradise*, there is not a trace of sentimentality in his description. And this self-discipline, akin to the stoicism of the sagas, is his ultimate response to the Icelandic landscape.

II   Love is Enough *(1872)*

Love is Enough; Or, The Freeing of Pharamond is both a love quest in the romantic tradition of Shelley's *Alastor* and Keats' *Endymion* and the first of Morris' imaginative works to reflect his experience of Iceland.[3] As such, it performs the transition between the two major phases of Morris' writing. Akin to *Earthly Paradise* figures like the protagonists of "The Watching of the Falcon" and "The Land East of the Sun and West of the Moon," the quester-king Pharamond also foreshadows the heroes of Morris' later romances. And while the tone of the poem shares the complex "heart-sickness" of "The Hill of Venus"—which Morris found he could not escape even in the bare wilderness of Iceland—*Love is Enough* gropes toward the affirmation of natural process and human struggle that characterizes the literary work of his final twenty years.

A ruler at the height of his powers, Pharamond dreams a succession of dreams about a maiden in a northern valley that drive him to leave his kingdom and, along with his foster-father Master Oliver, search for "the unknown desire / Of [his] soul . . . wrought in the shape of a woman" (IX, 29). After years of fruitless travel—the account of which (IX, 43–45) prefigures episodes Morris will develop in the late romances—he reaches the land of his visions and is united with Azalais. Then, in the final scene of his quest, Pharamond returns with Oliver to his old kingdom, only to find it in the hands of a new ruler. The tale closes with Pharamond contemplating his return to Azalais.

Like the *Earthly Paradise* narratives, the central fable is enclosed by an elaborate frame. Pharamond's story is the subject of a masque celebrating the nuptials of an emperor and empress who, together with the mayor, who acts as a master of ceremonies, and the peasant couple Giles and Joan, who have come to see the whole affair, offer concentric frames of commentary—noble, bourgeois, and rustic—on the events of his quest. Moreover, the masque itself contains three discrete elements: (1) a sequence of lyric poems designated "The Music"; (2) six scenes narrating Pharamond's discontent with his kingship, his decision to search for the maiden of his dream visions, the final stages of his journey, his meeting with Azalais, and his return to his former kingdom; and (3) the figure of "Love," who acts both as an interpreter outside the action and as a controlling force within it.

Like the narrative frame of *The Earthly Paradise*, this complex structure at once distances us from the heroic protagonist and suggests the variety of responses possible to his quest. We are not allowed to forget that the masque "Of Pharamond the Freed" is a "story/Wrought long ago for some dead poet's glory" (IX, 12), and that its performers may be just as important as—or even more important than—the legendary figures of Pharamond and Azalais. On the other hand, there is an inevitability in the dramatic presentation that the major himself attributes to "Love" (IX, 8, 83) and that is enriched both by the actor and actress assigned to the central roles being in love with one another and by the royal and peasant onlookers finding the tale and its performers apposite to their own circumstances. As an entirety, then, the poem suggests the conditions of "perfect" art, in which the interactions of historic legend and present events, of play and performers, and of stage representation and its audience are mutually supportive.

Despite the self-proclaimed artifice of his presentation, Pharamond is among the most intensely realized characters in Morris' work. Like Morris' own expedition to Iceland, his quest reverses the North-South itinerary of the Wanderers' voyage. Indeed, the valley in which he envisions—and ultimately finds— Azalais is girt by "a grey wall of mountains,/Rent apart in three places and tumbled together/In old times of the world when the earth-fires flowed forth" (IX, 24) that is distinctly Icelandic. "Twas not in the Southlands," he explains to Master Oliver, "for sharp in the sunset and sunrise the air is" (IX, 25–26). But whereas Morris' journey was a reaction from erotic failure, the aim of Pharamond's is erotic fulfillment. And this distinction is crucial, because it suggests the affirmative construction Morris himself was able to put on his expedition. If the failure of his marriage was Morris' failure to live up to the demands of his own imagination, then Iceland in reaffirming the validity of his imagination in a very real way reaffirmed the sources of his love.

However, Pharamond's erotic quest is also a rejection of kingship. The theme of private love versus public honor played an important part in *The Earthly Paradise*, but in *Love is Enough* it resurfaces with a new emphasis. For the "Freeing" that Pharamond undergoes is a release from the deadening influence of political authority itself. This revised perspective is clearest in this final scene of the masque, in which Pharamond returns to his former kingdom and contemplates its new rulers. He justifies his return as a "gift" to Master Oliver, but Love recognizes the hunger of Pharamond's imagination at work: "our one desire/Fulfilled at last, what next shall feed the fire?" he asks, and then goes on to summarize a collection of possible motives:

> Well, Pharamond fulfilled of love must turn
> Unto the folk that still he deemed would yearn
> To see his face, and hear his voice once more;
> And he was mindful of the days passed o'er,
> And fain had linked them to these days of love;
> And he perchance was fain the world to move
> While love looked on; and he perchance was fain
> Some pleasure of the strife of old to gain.
>
> (IX, 65)

The notion of a link is central. Pharamond is not attempting to relive the past, but to forge a bond between past and present—between the material world of kingship and the imaginative world of love. Like the heroes of the later romances, he returns to his society in order to integrate with it whatever power he has gained from the world outside his society. Moreover, the gesture is not merely a sign of his duty to his own people. It is also an attempt to integrate his own past—conceived both as his own earlier experience and as his participation in the collective *Geist* of his society—with his achieved present.

Admittedly, the gesture is a failure. But its presence suggests the structural format of the later romances in which Morris' heroes will be able to achieve the synthesis Pharamond merely contemplates. Seen in the context of his literary predecessors, Pharamond's return to his kingdom is distinctly different from Walter's attempt to return to the world after his sojourn in the Hill of Venus. Walter was no longer able to relate at all to the society with which he once participated.

Pharamond, on the other hand, is unable to reassume his former role because he has grown to realize its limitations. King Theobald and Honorius, the councillor who is the power behind his throne, are offered as alternatives to Pharamond's new life of "Freed" eros. But neither figure proves adequate: Theobald, because the most powerful king is limited by the mundane nature of his power—"for wert thou the crown of all rulers,/No field shoudst thou ripen, free no frost-bounden river" (IX, 73); Honorius, the more efficient ruler, for the dehumanization implicit in political realism—

> —Thou lovest not mercy, yet shalt thou be merciful;
> Thou joy'st not in justice, yet just shall they dooms be;
> No deep hell thou dreadest, nor dream'st of high heaven;
> No gleam of love leads thee; no gift men may give thee;
> For no kiss, for no comfort the lone way thou wearest,
> A blind will without life, lest thou faint ere the end come.
>
> (IX, 74)

Pharamond's decision to return to Azalais may represent an unsatisfactory resolution of the conflict between eros and civilization. Nevertheless, *Love is Enough* suggests that Morris was beginning to conceive of the issues in broader terms than he allowed himself in *The Earthly Paradise*. Specifically, that he has sensed the need to deal with the liabilities of political power and intellectual dominance that are to be a major concern of *Sigurd the Volsung* and the later romances.

This enlarged perspective is most striking in Morris' treatment of Love. Both the character Love and the singer of "The Music"—who is related to the speaker of the twelve *Earthly Paradise* lyrics—argue the possibility of confusing love with a contrary set of emotions. Referring to "those tales of empty striving, and lost days," Love insists, "never lit my fire/Such ruin as this; but Pride and Vain-desire,/My counterfeits and foes, have done the deed" (IX, 38). And the fourth recurrence of "the music" describes the poet's wrestling—Jacob-fashion—with what he takes for Love and vanquishes, only to waken to the discovery that

> *With a Shadow of the Night had I wrestled in vain.*
>
> *And the Shadow of the Night and not Love has departed;*
> *I was sore, I was weary, yet Love lived to seek;*
> *So I scaled the dark mountains, and wandered sad-hearted*

Over wearier wastes, where e'en sunlight was bleak,
With no rest of the night for my soul waxen weak.

With no rest of the night; for I waked mid a story
  Of a land wherein Love is the light and the lord,
Where my tale shall be heard and my wounds gain a glory,
  And my tears a treasure to add to the hoard
  Of pleasure laid up for his people's reward.

                                                           (IX, 47)

To vanquish and be crowned victor by "the Shadow of the Night"
appears to refer to Morris' having won Jane. His morning-after
discovery is that "real" love—as defined by the ideal passion of
Pharamond and Azalais—has eluded him and remains therefore alive
as his own desire. The otherwise metaphoric "dark mountains" and
"wastes" have a literal equivalent, of course, in Iceland. And the
transformation of emotional struggle into narrative art echoes his
Laxdale rumination, "whatever solace your life is to have here must
come out of yourself or these old stories, not over hopeful themselves." Interestingly enough, he seems to envision his suffering
transformed into a literary form akin to the sagas—for which he has a
precedent in Pharamond's fixation on a minstrel's tale that echoes his
own history (IX, 42).

   Yet Morris' identification of his narrative art with Love argues an
important revision in his concept of eros. *Love is Enough* replaces the
Venus of *The Earthly Paradise* with a masculine figure whose
succession of guises suggests a power at once more complex and more
pervasive than the embodiment of love in the earlier work. He
appears—sequentially—*"crowned as a king," "clad as an image-
maker," "clad as a maker of Pictured Cloths," "with a cup of bitter
drink and his hands bloody," "clad as a pilgrim,"* and finally *"holding
a crown and palm-branch."* The identity of this figure is the crucial
issue of the poem. Love's transformations parallel the stages in
Pharamond's quest, but the exact relation between the two characters is difficult to assess, for Love is at once an expression of
Pharamond's own personality and an external force to which
Pharamond is a willing victim. This dualism represents a significant
advance in Morris' thinking, since it enables him to depict eros as a
single ambivalent force, rather than as one term in an ethical or
spiritual dilemma.

   Encouraged by the poem's pseudomedieval format, Morris treats
the two-in-one nature of Love as a religious mystery. Throughout the

masque Love is characterized in Christian images of Apocalypse and afterlife. He speaks of "the many mansions of my house" where his followers may expect "A wedding garment, and a glorious seat/ Within my household." And he looks forward to their fighting beneath his banner "when the hosts are met/On Armageddon's Plain" (IX, 78–79). However, when Love appears *"holding a crown and palm-branch"* to speak the epilogue, his wavering declarations suggest at once the positivist import of this religious imagery and the incomplete resolution of Morris' thought:

> —Reward of what?—Life springing fresh again.—
> Life of delight?—I say it not—Of pain?
> It may be—Pain eternal?—Who may tell?
> Yet pain of Heaven, beloved, and not of Hell.
> —What sign, what sign, ye cry, that so it is?
> The sign of Earth, its sorrow and its bliss,
> Waxing and waning, steadfastness and change;
> Too full of life that I should think it strange
> Though death hang over it; too sure to die
> But I must deem its resurrection nigh.
>
> (IX, 77)

Clearly heaven is synonymous with "The sign of Earth" and immortality is participation in the "Waxing and waning, steadfastness and change" of natural process itself. Hence, the significance of Love's promise, earlier in the poem, that Pharamond "at last may save his soul alive" (IX, 23). *Alive* is the key word. The "Love" Pharamond—and Morris himself—hopes to find "Enough" is indistinguishable from the life-force of nature. To give himself over to erotic desire is thus to participate in the cycles of the earth, and it is on this account that Pharamond is radically unlike the Wanderers of *The Earthly Paradise* and the heroes of their later narratives, who seek fulfillment outside the boundaries of the natural world. (Thus, unlike the speaker of the *Earthly Paradise* lyrics, whose alienation from the natural world becomes more apparent with the passing of the seasons, the singer of "The Music" recounts a passion that "grew up without heeding" through spring and summer only to appear full grown at the time of harvest when "the leaf and the blossom in the ripe fruit are blended" [IX, 21].)

Admittedly, the tone of the poem is far from a celebration of natural renewal. In contrast with the *Earthly Paradise* figure of Pygmalion, who uses art as a means of self-discovery, Pharamond must come to realize that his quest for the "unknown desire of [his] soul" is a quest for death—both the death of his former self and death as a necessary fact of participation in the cycles of nature. He must "free" himself of the impulse to dominate his own fate—symbolized by his rejection of kingship—and place himself at the mercy of an alien natural world in order to undergo the dialectical rediscovery of his own capacity for love, without which Azalais would remain an image in a dream—as unreal and as unsatisfactory as Morris' own Jane. The emotional strain of this gesture accounts for the somber coloring of the poem. Nevertheless, Pharamond's pained affirmation, "Cruel wert thou, O Love, yet have thou and I conquered" (IX, 49), resolves the conflict between nature and the individual imagination at the heart of *The Earthly Paradise* and defines the problems that will concern Morris during the remaining years of his literary career: the strategies by which the imagination can gain strength through participation in nature without being reduced to a merely natural phenomenon; the means through which individual self-discovery can be coordinated with social integration.

III   The Story of Siguard the Volsung and the Fall of the Niblungs
        (1876)

A few months before Morris published his translation of the *Volsunga Saga* (1870), he set forth his feelings about the work in a letter to Charles Eliot Norton:

I daresay you have read abstracts of the story, but however fine it seemed to you thus, it would give you little idea of the depth and intensity of the complete work: here and there indeed it is somewhat disjointed, I suppose from its having been put together from varying versions of the same song; it seems as though the author-collector felt the subject too much to trouble himself about the niceties of art, and the result is something which is above all art; the scene of the last interview between Sigurd and the despairing and terrible Brynhild touches me more than anything I have ever met with in literature; there is nothing wanting in it, nothing forgotten, nothing repeated, nothing overstrained; all tenderness is shown without the use of a tender word, all misery and despair without a word of raving, complete beauty without an ornament, and all this in two pages of moderate print. In short it is to the full meaning of the word inspired; touching too though hardly wonderful to think of the probable author; some 12 century Icelander, living the hardest and rudest of lives, seeing few people and pretty much the same day after day, with his old religion taken from him and his new one hardly gained—It doesn't look promising for the future of art I fear. (*Letters, 32*)

"I had it in my head to write an epic of it," he continues, "but though I still hanker after it, I see clearly it would be foolish, for no verse could render the best parts of it, and it would only be a flatter and tamer version of a thing already existing."

What attracted Morris to the saga was not its restraint of emotion, but its restraint of verbal expression. And its example of "tenderness . . . without a tender word, all misery and despair without a word of raving, complete beauty without an ornament" had a profound influence on his own narrative prose. Just as Morris the designer sought to rediscover and sustain the handicrafts of the English "folk," he sought a similar rediscovery in his poetry. Here, the anonymous "author-collector" defines the narrative role for which Morris himself had been searching—one in which the individual voice of the poet is universalized by participation in a national tradition too strong to be emasculated by "the niceties of art." Significantly, Morris conceives of this "12 century Icelander" as a man in limbo, who achieves an identity by preserving the past in the midst of the changing present and as a necessary result finds himself suspended—like Kirkiubœ farm in the Faroes—between two faiths, one "taken from him," the "new one hardly gained."

To create his own version of this saga was thus an act of greatest importance in Morris' reconstruction of his self-image as a poet. The denials of purpose he expressed to Norton suggest the doubts Morris had to overcome before he could set himself to the task—as do the six years that intervened between his translation of the saga and the composition of *Sigurd.* It is likely that the imminent production of Wagner's *Ring of the Nibelungs*—premiered at Bayreuth in 1876— spurred Morris to complete his own version of the materials he shared with the German composer. Wagner had published the text of his four operas in 1853, and H. Buxton Forman sent Morris his brother's translation of *Die Walküre* in 1873, in response to which— without having bothered to read the libretto—Morris denounced Wagner as "anti-artistic" and expressed his horror at "the idea of a sandy-haired German tenor tweedledeeing over the unspeakable woes of Sigurd, which even the simplest words are not typical enough to express!" (*Letters,* 61). This refusal to consider the possibility of his rival's success signals the enormous importance of the saga to Morris. Yet the terms of his denunciation call attention to the problem he himself found difficult to solve—coming up with a modern language adequate to the profound simplicity of the saga.

In a letter written nearly a decade after the poem, Morris suggests the rationale underlying the experiments with language in his translations of the sagas and *Sigurd* (and also in the later romances): "Once everybody who could express himself at all did so beautifully, was a poet for that occasion, because all language was beautiful. But now language is utterly degraded in our daily lives, and poets have to make a new tongue each for himself: before he can even begin his story he must elevate his means of expression from the daily jabber to which centuries of degradation have reduced it. . . . Study early literature Homer, Beowulf, & the Anglo-Saxon fragments; the edda and other old Norse poetry & I think you will understand what I mean."[4] Morris' sense of the degradation of contemporary English is in keeping with his sense of the degradation of the arts of life as a whole. His attempt to create a new language is thus no more extraordinary than his setting about to design new tables and chairs. In both instances creation entailed a rediscovery of the past. To this purpose *Sigurd* is written in a predominantly Anglo Saxon vocabulary and relies heavily on Old English syntactic patterns.

However, as Anthony Ugolnik argues, "Morris is not a linguistic archaeologist whose mission is to unearth the archaic for its own sake." Rather, "he seeks to resurrect what he perceives as the innate vitality of Old Norse and creatively incorporate it into his 'new tongue,' distinct and separate from the bastardized linguistic medium of his own age."[5] Only a genuinely English epic—the literary from whose primary function is "to teach the nation . . . its own traditions"[6]—could effect this revitalization of the language. Assuming the kinship of the Germanic tongues (including English) and their literatures, Morris believed the *Volsunga Saga* ("the Great Story of the North") "should be to all our race what the Tale of Troy was to the Greeks" (VII, 287)—not merely an episode in cultural history, but the thematic basis for an evolving literary and artistic tradition. For *The Story of Sigurd* is not a translation of the *Volsunga Saga*—Morris had already done that in prose—but a nineteenth-century poem written for a nineteenth-century audience, in which he intended to develop the "realism . . . subtilty" and "close sympathy with all the passions" (VII, 286) he had found strikingly contemporary in the twelfth-century saga.

Yet Morris could not single-handedly reconstruct cultural history. Critics admired the work, but public reaction was far from enthusiastic. Compared to *The Earthly Paradise, Sigurd* is a difficult poem, written in a difficult language about men and women whose customs and world view differ radically from those of Victorian England. Moreover, its narrative—despite Morris' efforts to emend the "somewhat disjointed" structure of the saga—could not but have seemed diffuse or even incoherent to readers used to the organization of a three-volume novel. The failure of the poem to reach the popular audience for which it had been intended effectively terminated Morris' career as a poet. After 1876 he was predominantly a writer of prose, not verse.

In later years Morris boasted that he had stuck "very closely to the *Volsunga* in [his] poem of Sigurd: it is in fact the same story, modern amplification and sentiment excepted" (*MM*, I, 474). But he also drew on other Icelandic sources—the songs from the *Elder Edda*, which he and Magnússon had appended to their translation of the *Volsunga Saga*, and the shorter version of the tale that appears in the *Younger* or *Prose Edda*—as well as on the Germanic *Nibelungenlied*, from which, like Wagner, he took the closing episodes of the poem.[7] Morris' treatment of these sources is a complex subject; it suffices to observe that they posed two related problems: resolving the inconsistencies in the legend and giving it an overall coherence. His choice of title indicates a concentration on the figure of Sigurd absent in the earlier versions of the tale. Even so, his hero is not born until the second of the poem's four books and is killed before the end of the third. No central event, no single character is sufficient to focus the swiftly unfolding episodes of the legend. Consequently, Morris must substitute symbolic and thematic unity for unity of action.

The events of the poem are a series of rises and falls that suggest a cyclic dynamic akin to that of nature itself, and this analogy is confirmed by Morris's imagistic stress on seasonal change and recurrence. Book 1 ("Sigmund") opens with an account of the dwelling of "Volsung, the King of the Midworld Mark" (XII, 1). His great hall is the embodiment of order and beneficent power. Yet even the terms of the poet's encomium—"A rose in the winter season, a candle in the dark"—remind us of forces ever at odds with the warmth and light of human achievement. In the midst of the hall rises a mighty tree, the Branstock, symbol of the organic strength of the Volsungs and of their bondage to the natural world. The Branstock can participate in the life of the Volsungs because that life itself is most fully comprehended through natural metaphors. Their fate is a "seed" that "hath sprung, . . . blossomed and borne rank harvest" (XII, 13; cf. 39, 42). Near the end of his life, Sigmund envisions his family as a "tree" that "was stalwart, but its boughs are old and worn" (XII, 49). In place of the single tree that stands for a single tribe, Sigurd, "the wide world's blossom from Sigmund's loins shall grow" (XII, 50).

The events of book 1 prepare us for the birth of Sigurd. Sought as a bride by Siggeir king of the Goths, Signy, daughter of Volsung, accepts him as her fate. When Siggeir arrives on Midsummer Eve to take his bride, Odin enters the hall and thrusts a sword into the Branstock, a gift to whoever can "pluck it from the oakwood." Siggeir tries in vain, as do all the men present, including Volsung and his sons, save the eldest, Sigmund, who seizes it with little effort. Siggeir attempts to buy it from him, but Sigmund rejects his offer scornfully. Doubly shamed, Siggeir is now the enemy of the Volsungs. And from this day their fortunes—like the days of the year following Midsummer—begin to wane.

Having promised to visit his son-in-law, Volsung and his sons journey to the land of the Goths, well-knowing what fate awaits them. Siggeir's men ambush and slaughter the Volsungs. Sigmund, who alone survives, takes up a solitary life in the forest, biding the time for revenge. To him Signy sends the first of her sons, but the boy fails the test of courage and is returned to the court. Aided by a witch-wife, Signy changes shape and visits Sigmund in his cave. The child of their union is Sinfiotli. Sent to his father, he passes the test and grows to maturity in Sigmund's company. With Signy's aid they slay Siggeir and his children. But having avenged her father and brothers, Signy reenters the flaming hall to die with her husband.

Sigmund returns to the land of his people and weds Borghild. Years pass. Sinfiotli kills Borghild's brother in single combat over the latter's unfair division of spoils. The queen poisons Sinfiotli, whose body is taken from his father's arms by Odin. Having banished his wife, Sigmund marries a younger woman, Hiordis, whose former suitor Lyngi attacks her father's island kingdom to avenge himself for the loss of his bride. Odin appears in the midst of battle and breaks Sigmund's sword. The aged hero is slain, but Hiordis, bearing Sigmund's child and the fragments of his sword, escapes with King Elf, who finds her on the battlefield and leads her to his father's kingdom.

In his version of the saga Wagner fuses the figures of Sinfiotli and Sigurd as the Germanic Siegfried. Morris prefers a more diffuse narrative, in which the elaborate circumstances of Sinfiotli's conception lead to his anticlimactic poisoning by Borghild. The result lacks the dramatic tension of Wagner's epic, but it enables Morris to emphasize the crucial difference between the two heroes. Sinfiotli is trapped by the code of vengeance that led to his birth. He is a man of violence. In the most remarkable episode of his upbringing, Sinfiotli and Sigmund are transformed into wolves and endure a period of schizophrenic self-division—half raging beasts, half reasoning men. The experience is necessary to chasten the arrogance of both father and son. But it is Sinfiotli who gives way to the bestial more fully. Similarly, when Sigmund refuses the deed, Sinfiotli obeys Signy and slays her two children—his own half-siblings—"as a drunkard breaketh a cup" (XII, 36). Sigurd—the "better one than I am" Sigmund prophesies in his dying speech to Hiordis—is a man incapable of such brutality. Hence, Morris omits the episode—which appears in his prose translation—in which Sigurd commences his adult life by avenging the death of his father. *His* Sigurd is a hero of a new order that transcends the old code of blood guilt and vengeance.

And yet the problem of defining this new heroism proved elusive. Books 2 and 3, which treat the events of Sigurd's life, are named for two figures, Regin and Brynhild, destroyed by their contact with the hero. Regin, the master craftsman who acted as foster-father for Elf and his father Helper, assumes the same relationship toward Sigurd and in this role presents the most troubling figure in the poem. He explains to Sigurd that he is the third son of the dwarf Reidmar. Before the coming of the gods the dwarves had been the dominant race:

"And how were we worse than the Gods, though maybe we lived not as long?
Yet no weight of memory maimed us; nor aught we knew of wrong.
What felt our souls of shaming, what knew our hearts of love?
We did and undid at pleasure, and repented nought thereof."

(XII, 75)

The gods undermined the power of the dwarves by teaching them the "hope and fear" of imaginative perception. Dissatisfied with their lot and tormented by their newfound sense of guilt, the dwarves developed the arts of civilization, but at length were corrupted by their greed for wealth and power.

Journeying through the earth with Odin and Haenir, Loki maliciously killed Otter, second of Reidmar's sons, and the three gods were taken prisoner in the palace Regin had built for his father. In return for the life of Otter, Reidmar demanded the gods give him the gold of the Elf Andvari. Loki captured the elf in his underwater lair and forced him to give up his treasure—including a gold ring of special power. Andvari cursed the ring, and the effects of his curse began immediately after Reidmar accepted the gold and released his prisoners. Fafnir, his eldest son, slew him in the night and, changing himself into a dragon, took possession of the hoard. Regin fled, but hoped to avenge himself and seize the gold from Fafnir. To this purpose he allied himself with mankind, whom he taught the various arts of which he was master. They accepted his teaching, but forgot its source and attributed his gifts to Frey, Thor, Freyia, and Bragi (XII, 87). Nevertheless, he bode his time, awaiting the hero able to slay Fafnir and win him not merely Andvari's gold but the great wisdom his brother had for so long kept to himself.

Sigurd, of course, is this hero. And to the extent that Regin intends merely to use him to his own ends, the dwarf is an enemy Sigurd must overcome. But Regin is far from an out-and-out villain. For the dwarves as a race are victims of the desires implanted in them by the usurping gods. They are aborigines who have succumbed to the lure of civilization. Even their lust for power has its origin in the "hope and fear" of the future the gods taught them. Thus, lying behind the events of the poem is a mythic representation of Morris' own ambivalence toward historical progress. Without the gift of imagination, the dwarves live a happy but uninspired life. With it, they are destroyed by the boundlessness of their desire and the torments of their anxiety over things to come. Regin may be a self-deceiver, but he seems genuinely to believe that the power he craves is power to undo the harm the gods have wrought: " 'When my hand is upon it, my hand shall be as the spring/To thaw the winter away and the fruitful tide to bring' ":

> "and the songs of the freed from the yoke
> Shall bear to my house in the heavens the love and the longing of folk.
> And there shall be no more dying, and the sea shall be as the land,
> And the world for ever and ever shall be young beneath my hand."
>
> (XII, 88–89)

Interestingly enough, it is Regin who instills in Sigurd the ambition for heroic action he otherwise seems to lack. Until he comes under Regin's tutelege, the boy is content with his happy life in Elf's pastoral kingdom. At Regin's goading—and with the counsel of Odin—he wins the steed Greyfell. After two unsuccessful attempts to forge a sword worthy of the hero, Regin is compelled to reforge the shards of Sigmund's sword. In a parallel episode in Wagner's *Ring*, Siegfried takes over the smithy and does his own forging. But Morris' Sigurd cannot so easily dispense with Regin. Moreover, we learn that it was Regin who made the sword in the first place—although the circumstances remain tantalizingly unexplained.

Regin knows he will someday be slain by "the sword in the hands of a stripling" (XII, 87). Thus, he suspects that Sigurd will kill him, and so his encouragement of the hero has a self-destructive element strangely at odds with his plans for restoring a golden age. Similarly, although Morris often paints him as a duplicitous self-seeker, there are instances in the narrative when Regin achieves an inescapably tragic stature. To Fafnir Reidmar gave fearless brute strength, to Otter restless cunning,

"And to me, the least and the youngest, what gift for the slaying of ease?
Save the grief that remembers the past, and the fear that the future sees;
And the hammer and fashioning-iron, and the living coal of fire;
And the craft that createth a semblance, and fails of the heart's desire;
And the toil that each dawning quickens and the task that is never done;
And the heart that longeth ever, nor will look to the deed that is won."
(XII, 76)

Regin is given the gifts of the artist along with a profound awareness of the inadequacy of art. Furthermore, Morris links this awareness with sexual inadequacy: " 'I toiled and I toiled; and fair grew my father's house;/But writhen and foul were the hands that made it glorious;/And the love of women left me, and the fame of sword and shield.' "

Regin, the artisan who longs to return to a pretechnological golden age—the artist who finds that his work has not compensated for but rather intensified his sense of loss—is akin to Morris himself. Regin is not the hero of a new epoch, but a necessary agent of the hero's coming-of-age who, like Morris' later representation of himself as the narrator of *News from Nowhere*, belongs too much to the world he seeks to replace to be able to accomplish the transition himself. And like the artists in Morris' earlier writing, Regin is a figure with whom Morris found it difficult to come to terms. By focusing a substantial portion of the poem on Regin, he emphasizes the character in a manner unprecedented by his sources. Moreover, his treatment of Regin suggests issues of good and evil, justice and injustice that might have given the poem profounder meaning had he chosen to work out their implications. But Morris' fascination with Regin was countered by his reluctance to commit himself to the character. Having slain Fafnir and tasted the dragon's blood, Sigurd is granted the "wisdom" to penetrate the subterfuges of his fosterer. He slays Regin in his sleep—an act explained by the warning that Regin will awaken with superhuman power, but nevertheless out-of-keeping with Sigurd's normal conduct—and thus rids Morris of the problem of dealing any further with a being who threatened to wreak havoc with the simple morality of his "Northern Epic."

In the final episode of book 2, Sigmund ascends Hindfell and, penetrating the wall of fire that encircles the mountain's summit, wakens the sleeping Valkyrie Brynhild. He gives her Andvari's ring and they swear oaths of eternal fidelity to one another. From this point in the poem one becomes increasingly aware of unsolved difficulties. Book 3 ("Brynhild") moves from the clear light of Hindfell to the "cloudy" kingdom of the Niblungs, with whom Sigurd is destined to accomplish his fate. Gudrun, daughter of the Niblung King Guiki, dreams a prophetic dream—indicating her future marriage with a glorious hero—and journeys to Lymdale to ask Brynhild's advice. The uncertain relationship between this figure—the daughter of a neighboring king—and the Valkyrie on Hindfell can be blamed on Morris' sources, in which they are two separate characters, but he has done little to remedy the incoherence of the original narrative. Sigurd appears at Lymdale and reencounters Brynhild. However, the scene simply reenacts their initial meeting; it is not a further stage in the development of their relationship.

Influenced by nineteenth-century philological theory, Morris envisions Sigurd as a solar deity whose inevitable setting takes place amid the "cloudy" Niblungs. But mythology does not solve the problem of depicting ideal heroism in action. Together with the two sons of Guiki—Gunnar and Hogni—Sigurd undertakes various exploits. But we learn of them only in summary, and most often Morris resorts to secondhand reportage. He tells us of the "song of the fair-speech-masters" who "sing of the golden Sigurd and the face without a foe" (XII; 158). Or of "his fame . . .

far abroad,
The helper, the overcomer, the righteous sundering sword;
The loveliest King of the King-folk, the man of sweetest speech,

Whose ear is dull to no man that his helping shall beseech;
The eye-bright seer of all things, that wasteth every wrong,
The straightener of the crooked, the hammer of the strong.
(XII, 205–6)

Yet the actual events of the narrative suggest a man who is defeated of his life's purpose almost from the start. Grimhild, the wife of Guiki, gives him a potion that causes him to forget Brynhild. He weds Gudrun and agrees to aid Gunnar, whom he has taken as blood brother, in winning Brynhild as a wife. Brynhild meanwhile has established herself in a hall guarded by another wall of flame. Only Sigurd can reach her. Through Grimhild's magic, the two men change shapes and Sigurd gains a bride for his friend. But when Brynhild comes to join the Niblungs, Grimhild's magic lapses and Sigurd regains his memory of the past. He attempts to make the best of the situation, but tension between the two wives mounts. In a moment of anger Gudrun reveals the true history of Brynhild's wooing. Brynhild demands her husband slay Sigurd. The Niblung brothers agree, and Guttorm, a younger brother absent when Gunnar and Hogni vowed loyalty to Sigurd, undertakes the murder. Brynhild subsequently stabs herself and by her dying request is placed next to Sigurd on his funeral pyre. Gudrun flees the hall of her kin.

For Morris the emotional core of the poem is the final confrontation between Brynhild and Sigurd in Brynhild's chamber. Together they recognize that they have been trapped by events beyond their control. Yet when Sigurd offers to put away Gudrun and take Brynhild to wife, she rejects his offer. The dramatic force of the scene is undeniable, and Brynhild's unwillingness to allow him to return evil for evil is in keeping with Sigurd's heroic identity. Nevertheless, the logic that forces Brynhild to bring about Sigurd's murder is alien to a modern reader. She seems willful rather than heroic. And what she perceives as submission to fate we are inclined to label evasion of responsibility.

Yet underlying the bleak ethical code of the sagas one senses a romantic myth struggling to assert itself. Two figures we saw in Morris' earliest writings—the sage-artist cursed with the inability to face "real" life, the young hero damned for his ability to face it—recur in the roles of Regin and Sigurd. In *Sigurd*, both sage and hero meet fates equally expressive of Morris' fatalism. Regin, master of experience, is corrupted by a mixture of cynicism and nostalgia. Sigurd, the innocent hero, is destroyed by his inability to cope with his own success.

The turning point of Sigurd's career—if we ignore his strange behavior toward Brynhild at Lymdale—is his drinking Grimhild's potion:

> He laughed and took the cup: But therein with the blood of the earth
> Earth's hidden might was mingled, and deeds of the cold sea's birth,
> And things that the high Gods turn from, and a tangle of strange love,
> Deep guile, and strong compelling, that whoso drank thereof
> Should remember not his longing, should cast his love away,
> Remembering dead desire but as night remembereth day.
>
> (XII, 166)

No simple draught of obliviousness, what she offers him is experience itself: "they saw the sorrow of Sigurd, who had seen but his deeds erewhile, / And the face of the mighty darkened, who had known but the light of its smile" (XII, 166).

To find a comparable transition we might turn to Shelley's *Triumph of Life*, in which Rousseau narrates his own fall into the world of experience, or to Keats's *Fall of Hyperion*, in which the adolescent Apollo takes on the burden of human suffering. Two very different analogues, but the implications of both are present—in unresolved conflict—in Morris' poem. On the one hand, absorption in the flux of natural events—"earth's hidden might"—separates Sigurd from Brynhild and brings about his doom. The "tangle" in which he finds himself is of a kind with the net in which Reidmar entraps the three gods—"so great that day was the Earth" (XII, 78)—and becomes a dominant image in the third and fourth books of the poem. It is a "tangle" from which Sigurd and the Niblungs are unable to extricate themselves. To discover the sources of primeval power is to be hopelessly overwhelmed by them. On the other hand, what Sigurd seems to drink from Grimhild's cup is an awareness of the suffering of his fellow human beings, and in this respect it is a necessary stage in his development as a complete man. Like Pharamond, he must give himself over to natural passion if he is to break through the constricting mold of his own heroism. However, the hopeful ambivalence of "Earth" in *Love is Enough* returns to a fatalism that differs from the outlook of *The Earthly Paradise* in its stoic reserve, but not in its philosophical pessimism. Thus *Sigurd* is not the beginning of a new epoch in Morris' development. Rather, it effects the final, cathartic statement of the poet's despair over the possibility of earthly happiness.

Whatever the implications of their deed, the Niblungs pay heavily for the murder of Sigurd. In the final section of the poem ("Gudrun"), Atli, king of the Huns, sends emissaries to ask for the hand of Gudrun. Her mother and brothers, awed by the Hun's power and flattered by his attention, seek out Gudrun and force her to accept Atli's proposal. As Atli's queen, however, she undertakes to avenge the murder of Sigurd by encouraging Atli's lust for the treasure of Andvari (now in the keeping of the Niblungs). The concluding episode of the poem strongly parallels the events of book 1. Atli sends for his brother-in-law, and, despite negative prognostications, they accept his invitation. Once within his hall, they are attacked by Atli's forces who, while Gudrun looks on impassively, eventually overwhelm them by sheer numbers. When only Gunnar and Hogni remain alive, they are taken prisoner. Atli demands the gold—unaware that Hogni had cast it back to the waters. Gunnar agrees to tell his captor its whereabouts if he gives him the heart of Hogni, but when he is presented with the evidence of his brother's death, Gunnar prepares himself for his own. He is placed in a pit of adders, all but one of which he keeps at bay by playing his harp and singing. Her brothers dead, Gudrun fires the hall of Atli—the third tribal hall destroyed in the poem—and kills her husband. Escaping the conflagration, she ends the poem by leaping into the sea.

Morris appears to have been fascinated with the Northern conception of Ragnarök—the catastrophic destruction of the world followed by the return of a golden age and the rebirth of Baldur.[8] Allusions to these events permeate *The Story of Sigurd,* and the "redeemer" (XII, 232) and "hope of the world" (XII, 223) undone by the malice and ambition of lesser men is a version of Baldur, "the perfect, spotless god . . . suffering the sins of others."[9] But Morris fails to effectively link the sacrificial death of his hero and the destruction of both the Volsungs and the Niblungs with any larger pattern of human suffering and redemption. Reference to "the sorrow of Odin the Goth" is the refrain of the poem. But just why the events of *Sigurd* constitute his "sorrow"—beyond the fact that the Volsungs are his descendants— remains unstated. The divine order intervenes at climactic moments in the narrative, but its actions fail to shape themselves into a meaningful design. Unlike Wagner's Wotan, whose moral tragedy informs the events of the *Ring*, the Odin of *Sigurd* is a force as unknowable as the fate to which he, as well as the mortal cast of the poem, is victim. The myth of Reidmar and his sons suggests a dialectic of historical progress through which the prehuman innocence of the dwarves might be synthesized with the disorganized imagination of the gods into a higher, "organized innocence." But this synthesis fails to occur. Thus, Morris' "redeemer" Sigurd is not a parallel—like Baldur—but an alternative to Christ; whatever his virtues, his death offers no escape from the essential tragedy of human experience.

Morris' ability to express this essential tragedy with unflinching stoicism accounts for the remarkable power of the narrative. Yet *Sigurd* falls short of success because its stoicism is at odds with its psychological realism. The more Morris develops the depth and complexity of characters like Regin, Sigurd, and Brynhild, the less we are satisfied with the crude imperatives of the saga materials. The more he implies a metaphysical rationale for the saga, the less we are satisfied with his refusal to develop the implications. *Sigurd* is a disappointment not because he overromanticizes the Icelandic saga, but because his fidelity to the saga inhibits the nineteenth-century poem he could have written. For Morris to consider *Sigurd* the crown of his literary achievement is only to be expected from a man prone to self-deprecation. It is the work in which Morris is least Morris, a literary mode at odds with his native bent for psychological verisimilitude. On the other hand, *Sigurd* carries the process of self-distancing commenced with the Icelandic journeys to its necessary culmination. Working in the mode of the anonymous "12 century Icelander," Morris learned the self-discipline missing in his earlier writing. From this point in his literary career, Morris was able to become increasingly comfortable with his own identity as a creative artist.

CHAPTER 5

"How We Might Live":
Morris as a Socialist

T HE 1880s were the busiest and, for many of his admirers, the
most important decade of Morris' career. From November 1883,
when Morris declared himself a socialist, he worked unremittingly on
behalf of the movement. He lectured in halls and demonstrated on
street corners; he traveled, he organized, he conciliated; he wrote
articles, reviews, and socialist romances; he gave his time, his money,
and his energy to the cause. And the result of these sacrifices was a
new level of greatness both in his life and in his writings. In his best
lectures, in *News from Nowhere* and the other romances, he speaks to
us with an urgency and frank sincerity that have not lost their power
to persuade.

I *Lecturer and Essayist*

In his appendix to *The Unpublished Lectures of William Morris*
Eugene D. LeMire lists one hundred and ninety-seven speeches and
lectures delivered by Morris during the last twenty years of his life.
Many are one-time responses to current events. Others were written
for multiple presentation or publication—some as individual pam-
phlets, some, together with his best journalistic prose, in the two
essay collections he made in his lifetime: *Hopes and Fears for Art*
(1882) and *Signs of Change* (1888). Often anthologized, Morris'
lectures and essays are among his most widely available writings and,
to some readers, his most important.

The earlier essays derive from Morris' concerns with architectural
preservation and his profession as a designer. However, even the first
of his public lectures, "The Decorative Arts" (1877)—published as
"The Lesser Arts"—assumes Ruskin's premise that the discussion of
art is inseparable from the discussion of society as a whole. "In my

111

mind," he explained two years later in "The Art of the People," "it is not possible to dissociate art from morality, politics, and religion" (XXII, 47). For "real art" is "the expression of man's happiness in his labour" (XXII, 46) and its function is to offer like happiness to the men who come in contact with it. "To give people pleasure in the things they must perforce use, that is the great office of decoration; to give people pleasure in the things they must perforce *make,* that is the other use of it" (XXII, 5). From this double proposition—and the belief that what was true for "decoration" was true for all art—Morris' program for the renewal of art and society logically and inevitably follows.

By the early 1880s Morris realized that the art he envisioned could only flourish when maker and user confront one another as equals. The failure of nineteenth-century high art lay in the elitist notion of the artist's calling and the correlative assumption that art could only be understood by the highly educated—and only paid for by the rich. At the same time, the demise of craftsmanship could be traced to the low social status of the workman and the assumption that his work was—and ought to be—devoid of imaginative self-expression. Mutually alienated, artists and workmen lost their sense of purpose and wasted their powers on useless art and pleasureless manufacture.

For Morris this state of affairs argued the death of art itself. "Under the apparent satisfaction with the progress of art of late years there lies in the minds of most thinking people a feeling of mere despair as to the prospects of art in the future" (XXIII, 164). "The world . . . will one day wipe the slate, and be clean rid of her impatience of the whole matter . . . in all that has to do with beauty the invention and ingenuity of man will have come to a dead stop; and all the while Nature will go on with her eternal recurrence of lovely changes . . . ever bearing witness against man that he has deliberately chosen ugliness instead of beauty, and to live where he is strongest amidst squalor or blank emptiness" (XXII, 10–11). This theme runs through Morris' correspondence in the early 1880s. "The arts have got to die, what is left of them, before they can be born again," he wrote with a mixture of despondency and cautious hope to Georgiana Burne-Jones (*Letters,* 180). His despair over the state of nineteenth-century art turned Morris into a revolutionary. For he realized that the achievements of individuals—like himself—were not enough: "A reform in art which is founded on individualism must perish with the individuals who have set it going" (*Letters,* 187). Instead, the rebirth of art must come from the people. Turning to history, it seemed to him that all great periods of art had their roots in folk culture: specifically, in the pleasures of making and using ordinary things—ceramics, textiles, household utensils. Hence, Morris' repeated emphasis on the proposition that "nothing can be a work of art which is not useful" (XXII, 23).

The injunction is deliberately overstated. It is meant to be revolutionary. The point is not that Morris undervalued high art,[1] but that he believed the high arts could only be reborn after a period in which the "lesser arts" held sway over the imagination. Moreover, "usefulness"—which he extends to whatever is able to "minister to the body when well under command of the mind, or . . . amuse, soothe, or elevate the mind in a healthy state" (XXII, 23)—is a criterion that bridges the gap between social classes. Morris knew very well that working-class Englishmen of his day could not be expected to appreciate high art. "Let us once for all get rid of the idea of the mass of people having an intuitive idea of Art," he cautioned an 1891 audience, "unless they are in immediate connection with the great traditions of times past, and unless they are every day meeting with things that are beautiful and fit" (*MM*, I, 307–8). Art will only give pleasure to the mass of ordinary men and women if ordinary men and women are given a good education—specifically, are taught to reverence and love the past of their own nation—and are allowed to live in naturally and architecturally beautiful surroundings.

Thus, Morris' view of the function of art took him in two important directions: toward altering the conditions of the worker so that his labor will indeed be pleasure, and toward altering the conditions of life so that all men and women will be able to respond to the beauty of art. The first led directly to the obliteration of social classes and—whenever possible—of the factory system; the second, to an ecological awareness of surprising contemporaneity. We have "time enough and to spare" to advance the causes of science and technology, he warns us in "The Prospects of Architecture" (1881),

time enough for subduing all the forces of nature to our material wants: but no time to spare before we turn our eyes and our longing to the fairness of the earth; lest the wave of human need sweep over it and make it not a hopeful desert as it once was, but a hopeless prison; lest man should find at last that he has toiled and striven, and conquered, and set all things on the earth under his feet, that he might live thereon himself unhappy. (XXII, 120)

But Morris is no machine-breaker. He realizes that the primary danger of technology is ideological, not aesthetic: "it is the allowing of our machines to be our masters and not our servants that so injures the beauty of life nowadays" (XXIII, 24).

If "luxury"—the superabundant gratification of "material wants"—is the enemy of art (XXII, 48, 75), then we must instead cultivate simplicity: "Simplicity of life, even the barest, is not misery, but the very foundation of refinement: a sanded floor and white-washed walls, and the green trees and flowery meads and living waters outside; or a grimy palace amid the smoke with a regiment of housemaids always working together to smear the dirt together so that it may be unnoticed; which, think you, is the most refined, the most fit for a gentleman of these two dwellings?" (XXII, 149–50). *"Have nothing in your houses,"* he urges the audience of "The Beauty of Life" (1880), *"that you do not know to be useful, or believe to be beautiful"* (XXII, 76). Yet even this advice is not enough. In a passage that E. P. Thompson emphasizes in his account of Morris' conversion to socialism, Morris admits

when we come to look the matter in the face, we cannot fail to see that even for us with all our strength it will be a hard matter to bring about that birth of the new art; for between us and that which is to be, if art is not to perish utterly, there is something alive and devouring; something as it were a river of fire that will put all that tries to swim across to a hard proof indeed, and scare from the plunge every soul that is not made fearless by desire of truth and insight of the happy days to come beyond. (XXII, 131)

Socialism gave Morris a causal explanation for the sorry state of Victorian art. Marx's economics explained the necessary existence of the social inequality that had for so long disturbed him. It also explained why goods manufactured for commerce had given the death blow to British artisanship. If the end of labor was no longer use but profit, then the workman no longer functioned in a cooperative relationship with the consumer. "It is frivolous to consider whether the wares when made will be of more or less use to the world so long as any one can be found to buy them at a price which, when the workman engaged in making them has received of necessaries and comforts as little as he can be got to take, will leave something over as a reward to the capitalist who has employed him" (XXIII, 180). And it is "this superstition of commerce being an end in itself, of man made for commerce, not commerce for man, of which art has sickened" (XXIII, 180). Perceived in this frame of reference, the rebirth of art does not merely entail bringing about social equality and ameliorating the conditions of labor. It demands a rejection of the commercial system on which British wealth and military supremacy had come to depend. This was the "river of fire" Morris had the courage to swim.

Having passed the ordeal, the essays Morris wrote as a declared socialist were directed to two general concerns: laying bare the abuses of the capitalist system and setting forth the advantages of the socialist. The latter was Morris' distinct contribution to the movement. In pieces like "A Factory as it Might Be" (1884), "How We Live and How We Might Live" (1888), and "The Society of the Future" (1888), he defines standards of human fulfillment against which any political or economic revolution must be judged. His minimal requirements can be summarized easily: "First, a healthy body; second, an active mind in sympathy with the past, the present, and the future; thirdly, occupation fit for a healthy body and an active mind; and fourthly, a beautiful world to live in" (XXIII, 25). But it was Morris' special gift to be able to imagine these abstract aims in full-fleshed realization. Life under socialism was not to be just a negation of wrongs—no more than what he meant by "a healthy body" was just the absence of disease: "To feel mere life a pleasure; to enjoy the moving one's limbs and exercising one's bodily powers; to play, as it were, with sun and wind and rain; to rejoice in satisfying the due bodily appetites of a human animal without fear of degradation or sense of wrong-doing: yes, and therewithal to be well-formed, straight-limbed, strongly knit, expressive of countenance—to be, in a word, beautiful—that also I claim. If we cannot have this claim satisfied, we are but poor creatures after all" (XXIII, 17).

In his advocacy of socialism, Morris took it for granted that the satisfaction to be derived from cooperation exceeds that of individual accomplishment. He had felt much the same when he dreamed of founding an Order of Sir Galahad. It was implicit in his reverence for Gothic architecture—the supreme example of art as cooperation. However, his sense of the failure of nineteenth-century art and his commitment to socialism resulted in a more fully articulated statement of this longstanding belief. The artists doomed to work "Under Plutocracy" are directly injured "by the system which insists on individualism and forbids co-operation. For first, they are cut off from tradition, that wonderful, almost miraculous accumulation of the skill of ages, which men find themselves partakers in without effort on their part," and at the same time they are cut off from their contemporaries, for "there is in the public of to-day no real knowledge of art, and little love for it. . . . Therefore the artists are obliged to express themselves, as it were, in a language not understanded of the people" (XXIII, 167).

In contrast, "when art was abundant and healthy, all men were more or less artists; that is to say, the instinct for beauty which is inborn in every complete man had such force that the whole body of craftsmen habitually and without conscious effort made beautiful things, and the audience for the authors of intellectual art was nothing short of the whole people. And so they had each an assured hope of gaining that genuine praise and sympathy which all men who exercise their imagination in expression most certainly and naturally crave, and the lack of which does certainly injure them in some way; makes them shy, over-sensitive, and narrow, or else cynical and mocking, and in that case wellnigh useless" (XXIII, 168). Applying the example of artists to the nineteenth century in general, Morris underestimated the yearning for healthy individualism bred by the factory system. His own individualism came so easy it was difficult for him to recognize that other men might not have longed as deeply as he for the assurances of cooperative effort—that it was the lack of individualism in the capitalist system, not its overemphasis, which was at odds with human aspirations. The broad terms in which he defines "co-operation" argue that his chief concern was liberating the individual, not constraining him. But Morris' concern with the role of "special men" in the late romances suggests that the ideal of cooperation in his socialist lectures was based on an oversimplification of human nature with which he never found himself entirely comfortable.

The other assumption underlying Morris' socialist essays is his insistence that work itself is pleasurable. Again, Morris' own summary says it best: "The pleasure which ought to go with the making of every piece of handicraft has for its basis the keen interest which every healthy man takes in healthy life, and is compounded, it seems to me, chiefly of three elements; variety, hope of creation, and the self-respect which comes of a sense of usefulness; to which must be added that mysterious bodily pleasure which goes with the deft exercise of the bodily powers" (XXIII, 174). Morris lived in a universe from which the predisposition to sloth had been banished: "As to the unreasoning, sensuous pleasure in handiwork, I believe in good sooth that it has more power of getting rough and strenuous work out of men, even as things go, than most people imagine. At any rate it lies at the bottom of the production of all art, which cannot exist without it even in its feeblest and rudest form" (XXIII, 174).

His assurances that all men really enjoy work—provided it is useful and performed under conditions that are not degrading—is perhaps overconfident. But his recognition of the problem of leisure is prescient. To "pay" workmen with time off is no gain unless the time can be spent to some active, pleasurable end. "What then shall we do with the leisure, if we say that all toil is irksome? Shall we sleep it away?—Yes and never wake up, I should hope, in that case" (XXII, 33). (On the other hand, he freely admits "if I were to work ten hours a-day at work despised and hated, I should spend my leisure I hope in political agitation, but, I fear—in drinking" [XXII, 115].)

As "co-operation," Morris discusses "work" in such an unabashedly personal fashion that it is difficult to argue with his premises. Here, as elsewhere, the voice that emerges from these lectures and essays is very much that of "a man speaking to men." Few literary spokesmen for revolution have argued in such down-to-earth terms. For Morris, socialism was not a matter of political theorizing, but one of the plain facts of human experience. He makes his case most cogently when he makes his audience most conscious of the complex, responsive personality behind his words. He is analytic without being obtruse, plainspoken without being condescending. And the result is the deep sincerity that characterizes the writings of his final twenty years.

II   *Reimagining the Past:* A Dream of John Ball *(1888)*, The House of the Wolfings *(1888)*, The Roots of the Mountains *(1889)*

"Romance," Morris explained in 1889, "is the capacity for a true conception of history, a power of making the past part of the present" (*MM*, I, 148). History is not a collection of facts and data; it is the imaginative recreation of the events to which the facts and data refer. Moreover, this recreation presupposes a love of the past; hence, a willingness to idealize it—since the act of idealization provides a common ground for the historian and the events he recounts. It follows that the proper historian is a romancer and that insofar as "making the past part of the present" entails a transformation of the present, the romancer-historian is an agent of historical change.

For Morris, historicism was a dead end. Not only was it impossible to free oneself from the limitations of one's own time and place in history, it was also undesirable, because the value of history depends on the connection between past and present inherent in the historian's own limited point of view. (We learn from the past precisely because we cannot help imagining it in terms of contemporary

society, that is, "making the past part of the present.") Thus, the
Victorian architects who attempted to "restore" medieval buildings
to their original state merely produced forgeries that were neither
medieval nor good nineteenth-century architecture. Instead of preserving the past, they obliterated the evidence of historical process
and distorted the idea of the Middle Ages by palming off modern
buildings for old ones. On the other hand, the presence of medieval
buildings, with all the accretions and ravages of time, was living
evidence of historical process—at once a reminder of the past and a
testament to the discontinuity of past and present.

"Romance" derives from our awareness of this loss; if the past is
recaptured, it can only be in a new form created through the synthesis
of past and present. This belief is founded on the dialectical conception of history that underlies Morris' mature thought. Examining
historical process, he explained in the lecture "Architecture and
History" (1884), we are confronted with "inchoate order in the
remotest times, varying indeed among different races and countries,
but swayed always by the same laws, moving forward ever towards
something that seems the very opposite of that which it started from,
and yet the earlier order never dead but living in the new, and slowly
moulding it to a recreation of its former self" (XXII, 298). Morris
developed this conception in the series of *Commonweal* articles he
coauthored with Bax, *Socialism from the Root Up* (1886–1887), in the
lectures on English history he delivered during the same two-year
period—"Early England," "Feudal England," "Art and Industry in
the Fourteenth Century"—and, with greater significance, in the
three socialist romances he published in 1888 and 1889—*A Dream of
John Ball, The House of the Wolfings,* and *The Roots of the
Mountains.* If "Romance" is "a power of making the past part of the
present," it is in these three works that Morris performs most
single-mindedly the "true" task of the historian.

In a dream vision, the first-person narrator of *A Dream of John Ball*
finds himself in fourteenth-century Kent at the time of the Peasants'
Rebellion. He is invited to join a throng of men who listen eagerly to
John Ball preaching revolution and tags along to watch them ambush
and defeat a troop of soldiers coming to put down the uprising. Later,
after he has joined the peasants in celebrating their victory, he is
taken by John Ball to the village church. There, where the bodies of
the men slain in the afternoon's fray lie in state, Morris and Ball pass
the night in conversation. As the moonlight grows fainter, Morris

recounts the historical facts that await Ball and his cause: The king's accession to their demands; their subsequent betrayal; Ball's execution along with that of the other leaders; the eventual success of the Revolt's aim of ending the feudal institution of villeinage; the development of the capitalist system and its abuses as a direct result of the freeing of the peasants from the land. The more he knows, the less sanguine Ball becomes. But as the glimmer of moonlight gives way to the glimmer of dawn, Morris exhorts him to take hope in the inevitable rise of a working-class consciousness, through which the significant aims of Ball's struggle will be realized. The dream ends and Morris finds himself waking to the "white light, empty of all sights" of his Hammersmith bedroom. Hearing the whistles "that call the workmen to the factories, . . . I grinned surlily, and dressed and got ready for my day's 'work' as I call it, but which many a man besides John Ruskin (though not many in his position) would call 'play' " (XVI, 288).

A Dream of John Ball is among the most carefully planned and subtly wrought of Morris' longer writings. Its title makes a double reference to Morris' dream of the past and John Ball's dream of revolution, both of which are subsumed in the larger dream of a postindustrial socialist future. Thus, the narrative "I" is both an observer and an active participant in the events of the dream. His encounter with John Ball—and thus, with a crucial episode in British social history—sharpens his awareness of historical process and of his own place in the evolution of the future. Reimagining the past with an awareness of the present is thus a necessary stage in the development of his revolutionary consciousness.

The narration balances Morris' uncanny sense of participation in the scene with his awareness of his intellectual distance from it. Significantly, the initial link between the nineteenth and the fourteenth centuries is architectural. Morris enters the past through an acute, particularized description of its "brand-new" Gothic church, "at once bold in outline and unaffectedly graceful and also distinctly English," which on closer examination "quite ravished my heart with its extreme beauty, elegance, and fitness" (XVI, 217–18). It is within this church that his final colloquy with John Ball will later take place. Thus it is both an entry and a point of departure from the Middle Ages. But while his dream opened outside the church, it closes within it. His act of imagination has thus deepened his understanding of the medieval consciousness—but without ever entirely overcoming his awareness of alienation from the medieval world. The sharpness of his perceptions attests to the "reality" of what he sees and hears, but there are instances, such as the conclusion of the battle, in which the narrator "looked as on a picture and wondered, and my mind was at strain to remember something forgotten, which yet had left its mark on it" (XII, 252).

Throughout the scenes of action, Morris treats himself with an irony reminiscent of Chaucer's self-portrait in *The Canterbury Tales.* " 'Thou art tall across thy belly and not otherwise, and thy wind, belike, is none of the best. . . . Look no more on the ground, as though thou sawest a hare, but let thine eyes and thine ears be busy to gather tidings,' " says Will Green, who later leads him "by the hand as if I were a boy" (XVI, 227, 242). Morris is not just indulging his native playfulness. It is important that, despite his superior knowledge of historical events, he is in other respects inferior to the men of the fourteenth century. For he, like John Ball, is in need of "a new set of words" (XVI, 257) through which to make his aspirations more clearly understood.

Ball is the spokesman for a medieval Christian version of communist theory. In his great speech before the assembled peasants, he urges them to rebuild society on the model of the church itself: " 'For I say to you that earth and heaven are not two but one; and this one is that which ye know, and are each one of you a part of, to wit, the Holy Church, and in each one of you dwelleth the life of the Church, unless ye slay it' " (XVI, 230). For Ball, the realization of this vision will come through fellowship. " 'Forsooth, brothers, fellowship is heaven, and lack of fellowship is hell: fellowship is life, and lack of fellowship is death: and the deeds that ye do upon the earth, it is for fellowship's sake that ye do them, and the life that is in it, that shall live on and on for ever, and each one of you part of it, while many a man's life upon the earth from the earth shall wane' " (XVI, 230).

John Goode points out that Ball's mistake lies in assuming that liberation from villeinage will necessarily entail fellowship—rather than increased competition among workers for work.[2] This mistake is the lesson he painfully learns from Morris' account of subsequent history. On the other hand, Ball's ideals of fellowship and freedom *are* the real aims of postindustrial communism. And this dialectical relationship between past and future is Morris' own lesson from the dream vision. Even as Ball is speaking to the peasants, "I pondered all these things, and how men fight and lose the battle, and the thing that they fought for comes about in spite of their defeat, and when it comes turns out not to be what they meant, and other men have to fight for what they meant under another name" (XVI, 231–32).

Ball's belief that "heaven and earth are not two but one" errs because it is grounded on Christian theology rather than a secular interpretation of social change. Even so, the notion of "one" heaven and earth prefigures the socialist utopia to be brought about through the materialist philosophy that directs men to look for happiness in the world around them. " 'The Fellowship of Men shall endure, however many tribulations it may have to wear through,' " Morris promises his interlocutor, drawing an analogy to the light of dawn that has replaced the light of the setting moon:

"Lo you, an image of the times to betide the hope of the Fellowship of Men. Yet forsooth, it may well be that this bright day of summer which is now dawning upon us is no image of the beginning of the day that shall be; but rather shall that day-dawn be cold and grey and surly; and yet by its light shall men see things as they verily are, and no longer enchanted by the gleam of the moon and the glamour of the dreamtide. By such grey light shall wise men and valiant souls see the remedy, and deal with it, a real thing that may be touched and handled, and no glory of the heavens to be worshipped from afar off." (XVI, 284–85)

Waking to the "white light" of common day, Morris looks out at the Thames: "it was nearly dead ebb, and there was a wide space of mud on each side of the hurrying stream, driven on the faster as it seemed by the push of the south-west wind" (XVI, 287). The immediate effect of his dream vision is to heighten his awareness of the ugliness of the Victorian city around him, but at the same time it also gives him an intimation of the forces working for its transformation. The imagery of wind and tide is more than a figure of speech. Historical and natural processes are aspects of a single gradually unfolding phenomenon. Morris can "grin surlily" at the sound of the factory whistles because he has learned to place his individual efforts within the framework of an inevitable development for the fulfillment of which they—as well as the factory "hooters"—are alike necessary.

Morris could not have read Frederick Engels' *Origin of the Family, Private Property and the State;*[3] however, he was familiar with the book's central argument—echoed in *Socialism from the Root Up*—and may have read the work on which Engels' study is based, the American anthropologist Lewis Henry Morgan's *Ancient Soci-*

ety.[4] Engels—following Morgan—traces the evolution and break up of the system of primitive communism based on the gens (a clan or "family" tracing its origins to a single ancestor and forbidding marriage between its own members). Engels' interest in Morgan did not merely derive from Morgan's account of the gens system, but from his emphasis on the dialectical continuity of the values of the gens. To this purpose, his *Origin* concludes with a quotation from Morgan in which the anthropologist enumerates the characteristics of "the next higher plane of society"—"Democracy . . . brotherhood . . . equality . . . universal education"—and argued these *"will be a revival, in a higher form, of the liberty, equality and fraternity of the ancient gentes."*[5]

This pattern of loss and recovery "in a higher form" reiterates the historical dialectic Morris set forth in *A Dream of John Ball.* And like the Christian consciousness of the romance, the primitive consciousness of Morgan's gens held within it the seeds of its own demise. Morgan divides history into three stages: savagery, barbarism, and civilization. It is the second, which saw the full flowering of gens society, that Morris found most intriguing. In *Socialism from the Root Up* Morris and Bax followed Morgan's lead and divided barbarism into lower, middle, and upper conditions, which they then identified with the gens, the tribe, and the people. "Within the Gens, wealth was common to all its members, without it wealth was the prize of war." It follows that "this condition of war necessarily developed leadership amongst men" and then that the greater apportionment of wealth to the more successful warrior leaders led inevitably to some form of individual ownership. The tribe, which replaces the gens, is "a larger and more artificial group, in which blood relationship was conventionally assumed." While there was "by no means mere individual ownership," nevertheless "Communism had been broken into" and class society had begun. "The Tribe in its turn melted into a larger and still more artificial body, the People—a congeries of many tribes" which "held in it something more than mere *germs* of feudalism." Morris' two Germanic romances are directly related to the turning points in this scheme. *The House of the Wolfings* explores the transition between gens and tribe; *The Roots of the Mountains,* between tribe and people.

The plot of *The House of the Wolfings* is straightforward: Threatened by Roman legions, the gentes of the Mark unite under two war-dukes, the foremost of whom, Thiodolf, is the lover of a Valkyrie (Wood-Sun), who gives him a dwarf-wrought hauberk to wear in battle. Unbeknown to Thiodolf, this hauberk bears the curse that its wearer will be saved from harm at the price of his honor. After twice swooning in battle, Thiodolf refuses to wear the hauberk. He is killed, but the Romans are beaten and the life of the gens is preserved.

What appears in summary to be a clear case of the sacrifice of individual libido to the cause of a larger social entity, is, as Goode rightly observes, actually something very different.[6] Morris takes pains to have us realize that genuine life of the individual is inseparable from the life of the gens. When Thiodolf promises himself immortality in the life of his kin, we are meant to take him at his word: "if I fall to-day, shall there not yet be a minute after the stroke hath fallen on me, wherein I shall know that the day is won and see the foemen fleeing, and wherein I shall once again deem I shall never die, whatever may betide afterwards. . . . And shall I not see then and know that our love hath no end?" (XIV, 168). As he explains his participation in the gens to Wood-Sun, "I have lived with them, and eaten and drunken with them, and toiled with them, and led them in battle and the place of wounds and slaughter; they are mine and I am theirs; and through them am I of the whole earth, and all the kindreds of it; yea, even of the foemen, whom this day the edges in mine hand shall smite" (XIV, 170). And by becoming a legendary hero of his tribe—a Barbarossa or Arthur-figure, "not dead, but sleeping," ready to rise sword in hand "when the sons of the Goths are at their sorest need" (XIV, 207)—he does, literally, survive as long as the tribe itself survives.

The "House" of the Wolfings is at once a unit of kinship and a physical edifice. Like all the other gentes of Mid-Mark—the Hartings, the Elkings, the Bearings—the Wolfings are inseparable from their "great hall," "the Roof of the Wolfings." Morris' concern for the details of this structure is more than a symptom of his professional interest in interior design. "The Roof of the Wolfings" and its natural surroundings are an irreplaceable element in the identity of the gens.

They worshipped the kind acres which they themselves and their fathers had made fruitful, wedding them to the seasons of seed–time and harvest, that the birth that came from them might become a part of the kindred of the Wolf, and the joy and might of past springs and summers might run in the blood of the Wolfing children. And a dear God indeed to them was the Roof of the Kindred, that their fathers had built and that they yet warded against the fire and the lightening [*sic*] and the wind and the snow, and the passing of the days that devour and the years that heap dust over the work of men . . . for to them yet living it had spoken time and again, and had told them what their fathers had not told them, and it held the memories of the generations and the very life of the Wolfings and their hopes for the days to be. (XIV, 30)

Thiodolf threatens this "very life of the Wolfings" because he loves a woman who cannot be taken permanently into the Hall. As her name suggests, his meetings with Wood-Sun take place "outside" the gens, in the forest—that ambivalent world of natural potency that haunted Morris' imagination during the last decade of his life. As long as Thiodolf's loyalties are divided between Wood-Sun and the House, he can belong fully to neither. The events of war bring this issue to a head, but do not in themselves define the problem. Insofar as Wood-Sun belongs to an order of beings who are both immortal and of more than human potency, she suggests Thiodolf's romantic attachment to forms of permanence and power that limit his participation in the life of the gens. He is, in other words, threatened with a version of the individualism Morris deplored in nineteenth-century artists. Power and permanence of another sort are the rewards of full participation in the gens. Consequently Thiodolf does not forfeit them. As the "outside" figure of Wood-Sun is replaced by the "inside" figure of her daughter Hall-Sun (who preserves the sacred artifacts of the House when the Romans invade the Mark), he finds them in new guise—much as Morris himself was able to work out his "romantic" infatuation with Jane by transferring his affection to his two daughters, the stronger of whom (May) took an active role in her father's socialism. (As an adopted member of the gens, Thiodolf also bears a relationship to the Wolfings analogous to Morris' adopted kinship with the working class.)

Both war-dukes are killed in the final battle, and with the defeat of the Romans the kindred gather in the House of the Wolf to honor their fallen leaders. With this public act, the status of the Wolfing gens as *primus inter pares* becomes explicit. The war has united the gentes of the Mark into what is on the verge of becoming a single tribe, over which the strongest House is near to establishing its permanent dominance. But Thiodolf is dead. The man who might have made victory the occasion for establishing his lasting personal authority in the tribe is removed—fortuitously—from the scene. Thus Morris is able to maintain the integrity of the gens while at the same time making clear to us the agents and circumstances by which it will be superseded.

The Roots of the Mountains repeats this pattern of the hero's encounter with an "outside" world, but presents a more sophisticated differentiation of the "outside" into those forces that may be profitably integrated with and those that must be excluded from the society of the tribe. Face-of-God, eldest son of the house of the Face, takes to wandering in the forest that extends north of his tribal valley (Burgdale). He encounters an irresistibly beautiful woman (the Sun-Beam) and her brother (Folk-Might), who encourage him to forsake his former betrothed (the Bride) and lead his tribe along with theirs (the Kindred of the Wolf) in an attack on the Huns, who in the course of their migrations have displaced the Kindred of the Wolf from their ancestral home (Silverdale) and now threaten Burgdale. The Germans are victorious, and the tribes, united in battle, are further allied by the discovery of their forgotten kinship and by the marriages of Face-of-God with the Sun-Beam and of Folk-Might with the Bride.

Unlike the stark tragedy of Thiodolf's self-sacrifice, the denouement of *The Roots of the Mountains* is strikingly easy. Morris had intended to have the Bride killed in battle. But instead, as May Morris recalls, "She was spare to marry Folk-Might; 'it would be a very good alliance for the Burgdalers and the Silverdalers both, and I don't think sentiment ought to stand in the way,' " her father had explained in a letter (XV, xi). The alliance of the Burg and Silverdalers, which might have been limited by the Bride's death (for the Burgdalers resented her betrayal and were initially hostile to the Sun-Beam) or rendered less facile by devastating loss in battle, is instead a more-or-less effortless acceptance of the historical necessity propelling distantly related tribes into the formation of a people. Indeed, Burgdale culture embodies that "something more than mere *germs* of feudalism" Morris and Bax attribute to the closing stage of barbarism. While the role of the gens among the Kindred of the Wolf is still strong, among the Burgdalers it has degenerated into a system of prominent families, of which the House of the Face is unquestioned leader and its head, the craftsman-Alderman Iron-Face, the prototype of a guildsman-mayor.

The book's deliberate medievalisms suggest a shift in Morris' purposes from the simple historical reconstruction he attempted in *The House of Wolfings.* To some extent, the very strangeness of his first experiment in the genre—in particular, its heavily archaic diction and use of verse for important speeches—had emphasized the difference between past and present without engaging an imaginative counterresponse sufficient to "make the past part of the present." Moreover, Thiodolf's life-and-death dilemma is essentially tragic; he achieves participation in the gens at the cost of individual survival. In *The Roots of the Mountains*, participation in the gens is compatible with a level of individual freedom (not to be confused with individualism) missing in the more primitive world of *The House of the Wolfings*. The master craftsmanship of Iron-Face is a mode of self-expression unavailable to the gentes of Mid-Mark. Face-of-God is a younger Thiodolf, whose journeys into the wood are acceptable—although risky—gestures of self-discovery. And, unlike Wood-Sun, the Sun-Beam can marry into the tribe of her lover. The flexible, open society of Burgdale is thus close in spirit to "The Society of the Future," in which "the social bond would be habitually and instinctively felt, so that there would be no need to be always asserting it by set form" and "the family of blood-relationship would melt into that of the community and of humanity" (*MM*, II, 466). *The Roots of the Mountains*, in which "the family of blood-relationship" has begun the process of melting "into that of the community," dramatizes the elements of upper barbarism Morris hoped to incorporate into an ideal socialist society. So seen, the romance is a major component of Morris' utopian vision—an imaginary past that serves as his dialectical stepping stone to an imaginary future.

The optimism of *The Roots of the Mountains* is born of a reading of history through which the inevitable decline of gens society is a necessary stage in the rediscovery of the virtues of the gens in the "open society" of a communist utopia. Moreover, this pattern of loss and rediscovery underlies the structure of the romance itself. Its happy ending is not entirely a matter of succumbing to the allure of historical progress. Recognizing the inevitability of his son's wanderlust, Iron-Face offers Face-of-God permission to sojourn in what is now (in the fifth century A.D.) the decaying empire of the Romans. He suggests Face-of-God join the West-country merchants "and look on the Plain and its Cities, and take and give with the stranger" (XV, 20). No longer the directly aggressive force it appeared in *The House of the Wolfings*, the Roman world has taken on the more sinister form of a social order defined exclusively by buying and selling. Repudiating Rome and its values, Face-of-God chooses instead "the dark cold wood, wherein abide but the beasts and the Foes of the Gods" (XV, 19). Both symbolically and literally, he rejects civilization in favor of an earlier stage in the development of his own tribe (confirmed by the purer gens system of the Kindred of the Wolf) and, so doing, renews its spirit, otherwise weakened by the enfeebling charms of a good life in the valley. Thus, *The Roots of the Mountains* deliberately revises the historical paradigm set forth in Engels' *Origin of the Family, Private Property and the State.* How would northern Europe have developed, Morris seems to be asking, if it had not fallen prey to the enticements of Graeco-Roman civilization? Face-of-God answers this question by turning his back on the Mediterranean world and choosing the future the real Goths rejected, and as a result the society of the Burgdalers and their kin has a direct relationship with that of *News from Nowhere*, in which the values of the gens are rediscovered by revolutionary communism.

III   News from Nowhere *(1890)*

News from Nowhere comes closest to qualifying as the central work in Morris' career. Its portrait of daily life in a communist utopia summarizes his political and aesthetic aspirations. And its literary mode—the dream vision—connects them both with the medievalism of his earlier writings and with the prose romances of his final decade. But *News from Nowhere* is not the ultimate synthesis of his thinking for which it is sometimes taken. To read it as his "final statement" on any issue is a mistake. To ignore the book's shortcomings is to ignore the complexity of Morris' emotional and intellectual life.

In part, these shortcomings derive from the circumstances of the book's composition. Written to appear in installments of *Commonweal* from 11 January to 4 October 1890, *News from Nowhere* suffers from the inconsistencies and structural flabbiness common in periodical fiction. This was also the period in which editorship of the journal was taken out of Morris' hands. The month following its closing number, he left the Socialist League and founded the Hammersmith Socialist Society, thus bringing to a close his decade of intense political activism. The work is thus an effort to heal wounds, a self-justification in the face of failure, and a farewell to the decisive epoch of his life.

The opening chapter of *News from Nowhere* captures the atmosphere of a Socialist League meeting during this last year:

there were six persons present, and consequently six sections of the party were represented, four of which had strong but divergent Anarchist opinions. One of these sections, says our friend, a man whom he knows very well indeed, sat almost silent at the beginning of the discussion, but at last got drawn into it, and finished by roaring out very loud, and damning all the rest for fools; after which befell a period of noise, then a lull, during which the aforesaid section, having said good-night very amicably, took his way home by himself to a western suburb. (XVI, 3).

The suburb is Hammersmith, "the aforesaid section" Morris himself. And the position of the episode suggests that it was as much the Socialist League as capitalist society against which Morris' utopia was directed. On the other hand, the rhetoric of the passage attempts to defuse his criticism of the League with a comic representation of his own irascibility—and the (misleading) suggestion that he is more to blame for its disorder than anyone else. Nevertheless, the figure who emerges is that of a man who, despite this effort to be "amicable," must finally take his own way "by himself."

The conflicting intentions of the opening chapter characterize the work as a whole. News from Nowhere attempts to conciliate the anarchists by showing how far in their direction he was willing to go and at the same time reasserts Morris' individual vision in direct challenge to the hostility of the League. And both impulses led to exaggeration. His effort to dissociate social order from executive and judicial structures encouraged Morris to portray a society so lacking in structure that one wonders how its simplest affairs are managed. His need to vindicate a highly personal set of desires fostered a subjectivism that from time to time borders on idiosyncrasy.

Yet another special circumstance to consider was the surge of popular interest in Edward Bellamy's Looking Backward, which Morris reviewed in Commonweal (June 1889) and to which the early chapters of News from Nowhere were written as a point-by-point alternative. Morris was disturbed by Bellamy's version of socialism on several grounds. By portraying a future in which the gradual consolidation of business trusts has done away with private enterprise, Looking Backward challenged Morris' conviction that class war was a necessary stage in the evolution of communism. Similarly, Bellamy's concept of a "workers army" in which all able-bodied men performed the work of production challenged Morris' belief "that the true incentive to useful and happy labour must be pleasure in the work itself" (MM, II, 506). In matters of judgment, his glorification of urban life was at odds with Morris' dislike of cities; and his general content with nineteenth-century culture, unthinkable for a man who proclaimed that "the leading passion of my life has been and is hatred of modern civilization"

(XXIII, 279). To Morris, the regimented order of Bellamy's year-2000 America was "machine-life"—a goal only possible by denying "that variety of life is as much an aim of true Communism as equality of condition, and that nothing but a union of these two will bring about real freedom" (*MM*, II, 507). In short, Bellamy's rosy vision was Morris' nightmare; the widespread interest in *Looking Backward*, a threat to the "real freedom" Morris so strongly believed in.

It is possible for a utopia to function harmoniously on two levels—as a political model and as an "expression of the temperament of its author" (*MM*, II, 502). But in *News from Nowhere* the relationship between these two levels is not always harmonious. As a result, the book's significant defence of individual freedom has been obscured by its expression of Morris' personal tastes for half-timbered houses and damascene belt buckles. And yet, of course, this obfuscation is entirely in keeping with the vacillation between self-assertion and self-deprecation that characterized Morris' personality. It is as if Morris deliberately softened the challenge of his work by disguising it in idiosyncrasy—just as he at once ridicules the Socialist League and then assumes the onus of his own criticism in the opening chapter of the book.

This psychological pattern has its counterpart in the divided structure of the work, which falls into two unequal sections. In the first, the narrator, apparently rousing from sleep, finds himself at the Hammersmith Guest House (built in 1962 on the site of "the lecture-room of the Hammersmith Socialists"). He goes out to bathe in the Thames, where he meets Dick, who is working as a waterman; then, after a communal breakfast, he is taken to what used to be called the British Museum. Here, he spends most of the day discussing the political realities of the new world with Dick's great-grandfather, Old Hammond, whom Morris hints is his own grandson. The shorter, more intensely personal, section begins the next morning, when the narrator, Dick, and Dick's lover Clara set out on a boat journey up the Thames to join in the Oxfordshire haymaking.

Superficially, Morris' vision of the future is an extension of the aesthetic principles of Morris and Company. Furniture, clothing, architecture, and the other details of daily life reflect his admiration for the Middle Ages. Sound craftsmanship is the norm and the pleasure of creative work—which includes all useful labor—accounts in large part for the happiness of his utopians. Moreover, their work is characterized by an integrity of form and function, along with a

delight in honest ornamentation, that together define the aesthetic of
the new age. Their clothing is rich, yet appropriate for an active life.
Even the houses they build seem "alive and sympathetic with the life
of the dwellers in them." Morris' intimate knowledge of arts and
crafts enabled him to depict this life-style in evocative detail. One is
struck again and again by his intense grasp of the physical essence of
things. He is not content, for example, to tell us merely that the food
was good. Instead, he places us directly at the breakfast table: "The
bread was particularly good, and was of several different kinds, from
the big, rather close, dark-coloured, sweet-tasting farmhouse loaf,
which was most to my liking, to the thin pipe-stems of wheaten crust,
such as I have eaten in Turin" (XVI, 15).

Through similar passages, Morris is able to suggest the general
quality of life in his utopia. And through his extended dialogue with
Old Hammond—and, to a lesser extent, with the other characters—
he is able to fill in the ideological basis of this life. In the chapter
entitled "How the Change Came," Hammond offers a detailed
account of class war (in the mid twentieth century) and, with the
inevitable victory of the proletariat, the natural withering away of the
state as it had come to exist under capitalism. His explanation of the
causes of revolution derives from Morris' study of Marx. His account
of the effects, however, offers us Morris' individual thinking at its
most provocative.

Like many other utopian writers, Morris rests his argument on the
fundamental "reasonableness" of man. Common sense replaces
governmental bureaucracy. Man's innate fairness obviates the need
for a legal system. But Morris is not primarily concerned with the
nature of legal and commercial transactions; it is the simple beauty
and fulfillment of their life-style that justifies his utopian men and
women. And for this it is essential that they voluntarily forsake urban
in favor of rural life. The "leisurely, but not stupid, country life" that
characterizes his utopia depends on the obliteration of the distinction
between town and country life: "The town invaded the country; but
the invaders, like the warlike invaders of early days, yielded to the
influence of their surroundings, and became country people; and in
their turn, as they became more numerous than the townsmen,
influenced them also" (XVI, 71–72). Underlying this expectation is
Morris' assumption that the love of nature is a common human trait
the liberated consciousness will necessarily rediscover. In other
words, that men freed from the self-defeating values of capitalism will

inevitably rediscover the natural and therefore permanent sources of human happiness.

This confidence in the restorative power of the country is akin to Wordsworth's similar attitude toward rural life, and reminds us that *News from Nowhere* is a work very much in the British romantic tradition. For Wordsworth, return to the Lake District was equivalent to a return to the psychic wholeness of his own childhood. And for Morris, too, utopian society rests on a rediscovery of childhood innocence and spontaneity. "Shopping" for tobacco and a pipe on his way to Bloomsbury, the narrator "felt as if I were assisting at a child's game." Later in the day Clara leads him to dinner by the hand "as an affectionate child would." To the narrator's surprise, the dining hall is decorated with "such curious pleasant imaginations as Jacob Grimm got together from the childhood of the world." "I should have thought you would have forgotten such childishness by this time," he remarks to his hosts, who respond with a discussion on the nature of art, which in turn leads to Hammond's summary: "it is the child-like part of us that produces works of the imagination. When we are children time passes so slow with us that we seem to have time for everything" (XVI, 102). Hammond thus accounts both for the notably unsophisticated art we encounter in *News from Nowhere,* as well as for the apparent timelessness of its life-style. But even the narrator cannot resist muttering "second childhood" when Hammond proposes a toast "to the days that are!" And surely his reponse is not uncalled for. Morris seems to be urging a dialectic through which the strengths of childhood are synthesized with those of maturity. But the characters he portrays do not always seem to have succeeded in attaining this ideal.

At least two aspects of Morris' utopia encourage this immaturity: its system of education and lack of a sense of history. Overreacting to the "boy-farms" of his own day, Morris does away with schools altogether. (When the narrator uses the word "school," Dick can only understand it with reference to fish.) Instead, children learn by following the impulse of their own curiosity. The more serious part of education concerns practical affairs. Fortunately "children are mostly given to imitating their elders, and when they see most people about them engaged in genuinely amusing work, like house-building and street-paving, and gardening, and the life, that is what they want to be doing; so I don't think," Dick explains, "we need fear having too many book-learned men."

What is difficult to accept about this "system" is not its anarchy, but its belief in the power of individual curiosity. For the children of *News from Nowhere* are more learned than their nineteenth-century counterparts. " 'Most children, seeing books lying about, manage to read by the time they are four years old . . . sometimes even before they can read, they can talk French . . . and they soon get to know German also . . . they mostly learn Latin and Greek along with the modern ones, when they do anything more than merely pick up the latter' " (XVI, 29–30). But if children learn by imitating adults, then why would they take an interest in books to begin with—unless there were sufficient "book-learned men" to serve as examples? Morris does not appear to recognize the seductions of a practical life. He rejects the humanist tradition, but seeks to uphold the open-minded reasonableness we can trace to its educational presuppositions.

The unreasonableness of his expectations becomes clearer when we take up the specific matter of history. " 'I have heard my great-grandfather say that it is mostly in periods of turmoil and strife and confusion that people care much about history; and you know,' " Dick explains "with an amiable smile, 'we are not like that now.' " And we are assured that men like Hammond, with a keen interest in the affairs of the past, are something of a rarity. In their May-Day commemoration of the clearing of London's East End slums, it is customary " 'for the prettiest girls to sing some of the old revolution-ary songs.' " Hammond finds it a curious and touching sight " 'to hear the terrible words of threatening and lamentation come from her sweet and beautiful lips, and she unconscious of their real mean-ing.' "

Oddly, far from being ignorant of history, the people the narrator encounters in *News from Nowhere* are strikingly familiar with the past. They have forgotten the details of capitalist society, but this is largely a rhetorical thrust at the vanity of the nineteenth century. On the other hand, they are well-versed in earlier English history; they know the lineage of kings and the historical associations of their architectural monuments. They share, in other words, Morris' fascination with the Middle Ages and his view of history as romance. Similarly, despite their dismissal of "book-learning," his utopians are fully as well-read—if not more so—as most of Morris' middle-class contemporaries. Doubtless this is precisely what we should expect from his ideal men and women. Yet his need to endow them with intellectual culture and an historical sense is plainly at odds with his ideological view that they have outgrown the need for history. In effect, Morris is at cross-puposes with his own argument. Human beings liberated to "healthy animal life" in the present moment have no incentive to learn history, and yet without it, they are both imaginatively inadequate and vulnerable to their own impulses.

In part, what saves his utopians from themselves is their reliance on the natural world. The haymaking celebration with which the romance ends—and from which the narrator, who fades back into the present, is excluded—suggests that the definitive gestures of utopian man will be regulated by the seasons. Earlier, Hammond had summarized this relationship in somewhat different terms: " 'We of these generations are strong and healthy of body, and live easily; we pass our lives in reasonable strife with nature, exercising not one side of ourselves only, but all sides, taking the keenest pleasure in all the life of the world" (XVI, 57–58). But there is little evidence in *News from Nowhere* of this "reasonable strife," and more of submersion in the presumably benign power of nature.

Indeed, Hammond's remark has the effect of calling our attention to the problem. A "reasonable strife with nature" is precisely what is missing in Morris' utopia. He offers a vision of the future in which the individual's freedom within society is gained at the cost of his increased dependence on nature—perceived both as an external force and as his own instinctual life. Morris could have avoided this trade-off. *The Roots of the Mountains* portrays a society in which the balance of opposing forces is successfully resolved without denying the conflict between man and nature. And its resolution is convincing precisely because Morris himself seems to have believed in it. Instead of the aimless wandering that characterizes the society of *News from Nowhere*, the Burgdalers' "strife with nature" limits them to a familiar and therefore racially significant geography. And the dangers of their good life in the valley are countered by a ritualized commemoration of tribal history very different from the empty songs at the East End.

Morris never entirely solved the problem of exposition in the first section of the work. The question-and-answer pattern of much of the dialogue clearly taxed his patience. In chapter 11 it simply breaks down into a series of speeches labeled "H" and "I," through which the characters are reduced to the counters of intellectual discourse. More important, perhaps, Morris never adequately defined his own relationship to the utopia. At times the narrator ("Guest") is a coyly disguised version of Morris, rejoicing in the fruition of his hopes for the future. At others, he is set up as a typical Victorian, ready to be toppled with amazement at the strange turn things have taken. Not until the closing chapters does Morris seem to have come upon the mode right for his purposes. Earlier in the narrative, Guest plays a largely passive role. Journeying up the Thames, he ceases to be the bemused visitor from another century and becomes instead the hero of a romantic quest. The goal is nothing strange or extraordinary. It is Kelmscott Manor itself, and the surrounding Oxfordshire countryside Morris held so dear. Thus his journey up the Thames is both a quest into the heart of English nature and a gesture of asserting his right to enjoy Kelmscott.

But the narrator fades the moment he sits down to take part in the communal feast of haymakers in the Kelmscott church. His quest fails; for a man of the nineteenth century, life at Kelmscott is at best adventitious. Morris is as cut off from the twenty-first century as he was from the Middle Ages.

The act of writing *News from Nowhere* confronted Morris with the problem of relating to the ideal society implicit in his commitment to socialism. It forced him to answer the question, What is it I really want? But it was not until the final section of the work that he hit upon the terms of a possible solution—his relationship with Ellen. Their first night out from Hammersmith, Clara, Dick, and Guest are invited home by Ellen's grandfather. Two days later, Ellen unexpectedly reappears to join the party. The narrator gets into her boat, and together they row the rest of the way to Kelmscott. From the first he is struck by her "strange and almost wild beauty." In the figure of Ellen, Morris comes closest to imagining the radical transformation of human nature that would necessarily follow from the achievement of his utopia:

I must say that of all the persons I had seen in that world renewed, she was the most unfamiliar to me, the most unlike what I could have thought of. . . . this girl was not only beautiful with a beauty quite different from that of "a young lady," but was in all ways so strangely interesting; so that I kept wondering what she would say or do next to surprise and please me. Not, indeed, that there was anything startling in what she actually said or did; but it was all done in a new way, and always with that indefinable interest and pleasure of life, which I had noticed more or less in everybody, but which in her was more marked and more charming than in anyone else that I had seen. (XVI, 182)

Morris' treatment of Ellen is not merely a new element in the book; it is a repudiation of the earlier chapters of his utopia, in which the women—and men—of the new world fitted without much trouble into the narrator's preconceptions of human nature. She, however, is something wholly new and therefore confounds whatever expectations he brings to her.

Moreover, Ellen is the prime spokesman for man's new relationship with the natural world. " 'Books, books! always books,' " she chastises her grandfather. " 'When will you understand that after all it is the world we live in which interests us; the world of which we are a part, and which we can never love too much?' " (XVI, 150). Leading the narrator to Kelmscott Manor, she "laid her shapely sun-browned hand and arm on the lichened wall as if to embrace it, and cried out, 'O me! O me! How I love the earth, and the seasons, and weather, and all things that deal with it, and all that grows out of it' "—a sentiment she repeats once more in just the space of a few paragraphs: " 'The earth and the growth of it and the life of it! If I could but say or show how I love it!' " (XVI, 201–2).

Ellen embodies the essential strangeness of the new way of life. In the final chapters of *News from Nowhere* Morris seems to have realized that the heart of Bellamy's arrogance was his presupposition that the men and women of the future would be so very much like himself. Ellen gives the lie to this comfortable delusion. Moreover, it is Ellen who gives voice to the vulnerability of the utopian society Morris has created: "I think sometimes people are too careless of the history of the past—too apt to leave it in the hands of old learned men like Hammond. Who knows? happy as we are, times may alter; we may be bitten with some impulse towards change, and many things may seem too wonderful for us to resist, too exciting not to catch at, if we do not know that they are but phases of what has been before; and withal ruinous, deceitful, and sordid' " (XVI, 194). Her solution is the wisdom of the narrator himself. But he cannot remain indefinitely in her world, and nothing guarantees that the lessons he teaches Ellen will endure beyond her lifetime. She is thus a vehicle for Morris' deepest misgivings about the possibility of his own utopia.

But Ellen's third and perhaps most compelling function is that of the goal of an erotic quest. She is the woman Morris wants but cannot have. Their relationship is curious. She makes ambiguous statements that could be taken as sexual invitations: " 'This evening, or tomorrow morning, I shall make a proposal to you to do something which would please me very much, and I think would not hurt you' "

(XVI, 188). His response to her is rejuvenation mixed with anxiety: "I felt young again, and strange hopes of my youth were mingling with the pleasure of the present; almost destroying it, and quickening it into something like pain" (XVI, 187). His anxiety, of course, is well-founded. The erotic consummation that would have enabled him to enter fully and permanently into the future fails to take place. Once more Morris uses a literary medium to project his sense of erotic failure.

Eros is not absent from the earlier chapters. Morris is taken with one of the three women at Hammersmith Guest House—so much so that he feels "a slight pang" when their hands part. And he is struck with the physical attractiveness of all the women he encounters, including Clara, whose appearance prompts Hammond's discourse on utopian love in chapter 9. But the narrator's libido is restrained by his anomalous position within the story line, as well as by the ideological bias of the first section. Guest is an outsider; in contrast with the fresh, youthful appearance of the utopians, he appears to be eighty years old. Moreover, the reader is directed to focus on the details of life in the utopia rather than on the individual psychology of the narrator. Indeed, the inconsistencies in Morris' treatment of Guest in these chapters encourage us to accept him as a narrative device rather than a realized character. But if erotic fulfillment was Morris' underlying desire, then the earlier chapters' concern with theoretical Marxism was functionally a repression of his libido. This accounts for his technical difficulties with exposition. It also suggests that his exaggerated individualism in small matters may have been a means of compensating for his larger repressions. And it may even shed an unexpected light on Morris' political activism itself. Instead of freeing him from the pangs of unsatisfied sex, it merely suppressed the problem—until, at the end of the decade, it reasserted itself in the guise in which it continued to occupy him during the final years of his life: no longer in images of self-indulgent despair, but in new archetypes of the hero's rebirth and erotic fulfillment.

CHAPTER 6

"Glad Animal Movements": The Late Romances

THE six romances Morris wrote in the last years of his life mark a
significant return to the form and subject matter of his earliest
prose. It is as if, having fought his part in the battle for socialist
revolution, he had succeeded in liberating his imagination from the
toils of capitalist society and thus recaptured, in a higher form, the
innocent vision of his own childhood. The result is a body of writing
unique in its own, and perhaps any, time: a fitting crown to Morris'
literary career.

I The Story of the Glittering Plain (1890)

Morris' decision to inaugurate the Kelmscott Press with the
romance he had composed at odd moments while he was writing
News from Nowhere indicates the importance of the work in his
literary development. With *The Story of the Glittering Plain* Morris
deliberately reasserted his identity as a storyteller detached from
immediate political issues. Specifically, he reasserted himself as the
author of the romance he wrote in reaction to the utopianism of *News
from Nowhere*.

The opening setting is Cleveland by the Sea, a tribal community on
the coast of northwestern Europe, which associates *The Glittering
Plain* with the two Germanic romances. Hallblithe of the House of
the Raven is betrothed to the Hostage of the House of the Rose,
wherein (according to the law of the gens) "it was right and due that
the men of the Raven should wed" (XIV, 211). They are to be married
on Midsummer Night—a date of particular significance for Morris—
but she is stolen by sea raiders. Hallblithe, who undertakes to rescue
her, accepts the invitation of a red-headed stranger (the Puny Fox)
and sails with him to the Isle of Ransom, base of "the Ravagers" who

137

abducted the Hostage. After various adventures, he joins the old man Sea-eagle on his voyage to the Glittering Plain, where he has been led by a dream to expect to find the Hostage.

Instead, Hallblithe encounters the daughter of the Undying King. Having seen his picture in a richly decorated book, she has induced her father to lure Hallblithe to her. He rejects her love, but now finds himself trapped on the Glittering Plain—a timeless land of eternal youth, which bears an inescapable resemblance to utopian England in *News from Nowhere*. With the king's grudging permission, Hallblithe attempts to cross the mountainous waste that separates the Plain from the rest of the world, but he fails. Returning, he builds a boat and sails back to the Isle of Ransom. Here, with the help of the Puny Fox and his magic, he regains the hostage and brings her back to Cleveland by the Sea. The Puny Fox, now Hallblithe's sworn brother, returns with them and is taken into the House of the Raven.

Morris may have intended *The Glittering Plain* to contrast with *News from Nowhere*,[1] but the similarities are more striking than the differences. Except for the political fact of the king—who, despite his authority, has little real effect on the daily lives of his subjects—the Plain is an analogue to Nowhere. Hallblithe reaches it by way of a volcanic island clearly modeled on Iceland—just as Morris reached socialism by way of his two encounters with the North. The Plain, alternately known as "the Land of Living Men" and, more sinisterly, as "the Acre of the Undying," fosters an economy with "no buying or selling" (XIV, 246). Its inhabitants enjoy absolute harmony with nature and near absolute freedom of action. And the result is utter childishness. (The king even calls them "children.") Without strife with nature, they have no reason for technology or social organiza- tion. In a state of complete sexual freedom, they have lost the ability to love. Jack Lindsay attributes the inadequacy of the Plain to the lack of "fellowship,"[2] but this lack is an effect not a cause: in a state of perfect harmony with nature, there is no need for fellowship.

Hallblithe rejects this pastoral nightmare ostensibly to find the Hostage, but the innervation of its life-style is cause enough for his flight. And yet fleeing he rejects nature itself. The rejuvenated Sea-eagle argues against Hallblithe's return in terms of the very "glad animal" life Morris espouses in his utopia: " 'As to what thou sayest concerning the days gone past and our joys upon the tumbling sea, true it is that those days were good and lovely; but they are dead and gone like the lads who sat on the thwart beside us, and the maidens who took our hands in the hall to lead us to the chamber. Other days have come in their stead, and other friends shall cherish us. What then? . . . Shall we curse the Yuletide, and cast foul water on the Holy Hearth of the winter feast, because the summer once was fair and the days flit and the times change? Now let us be glad! For life liveth!' " (XIV, 257). Life in the bosom of nature is mere survival; eternal youth entails loss of commitment to the past and thus of identity itself.

Yet, Hallblithe's first attempt to reject this life confronts him with a contrary image of the natural world: "it was to him as if the crags rose up in the sky to meet him and overhang him, and as if the earth heaved up beneath him, and therewith he fell aback and lost all sense, so that he knew not what was become of the earth and the heavens and the passing of the minutes of his life" (XIV, 279). Waking, he finds himself in a barren waste—"a narrow valley or cleft of the mountains amidst wan rocks, bare and waterless, where grew no blade of green" (XIV, 279). Near death, he is rescued by three elders (whom he also encountered in the first chapter), whom he leads back to the Plain. He cannot use nature to escape the Plain; nature does not enable him to overcome nature, save, as for Morris at Thorsmark, through revealing its inhuman essence. Thus, what ultimately saves Hallblithe is craftsmanship—the exertion of human will and imagination over and against the natural world.

To the King's Daughter, Hallblithe and the Hostage are figures in a book because from the perspective of her enforced innocence, the world of ordinary human experience is akin to a romanticized ideal. In this respect, she echoes Clara in *News from Nowhere*, who countered Hammond's view that " 'it is the child-like part in us that produces works of the imagination' " with the wish that " 'we were interesting enough to be written on or painted about' " (XVI, 102–3). But the King's Daughter resembles Ellen more than Clara. She needs Hallblithe for much the same reason Ellen needs Guest. Both men offer an understanding of human nature missing in the innocent worlds in which the two women must work out their fates. The King's Daughter—whose very anonymity suggests her need for the hero who will rescue her from her father's domination—embodies the fear Morris largely suppressed in *News from Nowhere*: that she, not Ellen, is the likely product of his "Epoch of Rest."

The name Hallblithe suggests the stay-at-home nature of the young man's heroism. Unlike Guest, he is more than happy to return from his excursion to Dystopia. As he makes it clear in the first chapter of the romance, he is no "Wanderer" in search of an Earthly Paradise.

Encountering three elders in quest for the Land of Living Men, he answers their desperate question " 'Is this the Land? Is this the Land?' " with uncomprehending laughter:

"Wayfarers, look under the sun down the plain which lieth betwixt the mountains and the sea, and ye shall behold the meadows all gleaming with the spring lilies; yet do we not call this the Glittering Plain, but Cleveland by the Sea. Here men die when their hour comes, nor know I if the days of their life be long enough for the forgetting of sorrow; for I am young and not yet a yokefellow of sorrow; but this I know, that they are long enough for the doing of deeds that shall not die. And as for Lord, I know not this word, for here dwell we, the sons of the Raven, in good fellowship, with our wives that we have wedded, and our mothers who have borne us, and our sisters who serve us. Again I bid you light down off your horses, and eat and drink, and be merry; and depart when ye will, to seek what land ye will." (XIV, 212)

Here, as in the Germanic romances, fellowship is inseparable from tribal identity. In this respect, Hallblithe differs from the perambulatory residents of Nowhere. Indeed, his speech reminds us that what was missing in Nowhere was the very tribal hall and territory that play so important a role here and in the Germanic romances—the symbol that at once confirms the tribe's relationship to nature and its essential difference from the merely natural.

And yet even within the terms of the romance Hallblithe's quest is something of a failure. He ought to have saved the King's Daughter. He ought to have learned to love a woman different from those of his own tribe; to have awakened her to full human experience and at the same time expanded the genetic—and imaginative—base of his tribe. Face-of-God's successive relationships with the Bride and the Sun-Beam in *The Roots of the Mountains* suggest the emotional self-discovery missing in Hallblithe's development. Confronted with a virgin in need of rescue, he can only flee back to the home and family from which he came. Thus the relative ease with which he regains the Hostage in the final chapters and returns to Cleveland by the Sea strikes the reader as anticlimactic.

Hallblithe's insistent monogamy is in sharp contrast with the sexual morality of *News from Nowhere*. But Morris' attempt to affirm the values of home and family is unsatisfactory because Hallblithe does not grow through his experience. He merely confirms the attitudes with which he started. " 'I seek no dreams . . . but the end of dreams,' " he explains to the Sea-eagle. But this hard-nosed realism is as disturbing in its way as the ideological purism of *News from*

Nowhere. The romance is merely a reaction against the utopia; it is not a viable alternative. Yet contrasting the two works lays bare the contrary impulses that haunted Morris in his last years. In the romance he gives way to the love of the past and its traditions we have traced from his growing up at Woodford Hall. In the utopia, to the hopes for future change that were an inevitable response to his experience of a society at odds with the values of his childhood. As we shall see, his later romances were the medium through which the interplay of these two impulses evolved to its fullest expression.

II   The Wood beyond the World *(1894)*

The Wood beyond the World attempts to compensate for the inadequacies of *The Story of the Glittering Plain.* Both are quest romances. Both confront the hero with an earthly paradise he must reject if he is to attain full manhood. And, like Hallblithe, Golden Walter is lured on his quest by a vision of the woman he seeks. However, unlike Hallblithe, he sets forth not to rescue but to escape from his first love—a wife who has proven unfaithful. Moreover, he seeks not one woman—initially—but two. And, finally, instead of returning home to Langton on Holm, Walter and his bride find a new life among a people wholly new to both of them. Walter is thus a more complex figure than Hallblithe. He is able to profit by his mistakes and redirect his love to a worthier object, and he has the adaptability it takes to function successfully in a new environment. By enlarging the hero's range of choice in these matters, the romance offers a structure of individual development missing in *The Glittering Plain.*

Preparing to embark on his journey, Walter has a vision of three figures entering a ship: a hideous dwarf, a fair maiden with an iron ring on her right ankle, and "a lady, tall and stately, so radiant of visage and glorious of raiment, that it were hard to say what like she was; for scarce might the eye gaze steady upon her exceeding beauty" (XVII, 4). Returning to his father's house, he sees the same three figures pass before him on the street and then disappear.

His preparations complete, Walter sails on his father's merchant ship, but the images of the two women remain in the back of his mind: "he might not tell which of the twain . . . were clearest to his eyes; but sore he desired to see both of them again" (XVII, 5). After months of travel and "chaffer"—which succeed in taking Walter's mind off his marriage—a messenger arrives to announce the death of his father, killed in the feud he instigated by sending his daughter-in-law back to her family. Walter takes ship for home, but is blown off course by a storm. Coming at last to an unknown shore—once more, Morris' description suggests Iceland—he and his men land on a mountain-girt plain. Its only inhabitant, an aged Robinson Crusoe, tells them of a savage tribe (the Bears) who live beyond the mountains and hints at something more he has experienced but about which he refuses to speak. Sensing it has to do with the three figures of his vision, Walter separates himself from his companions, crosses the mountain barrier, and finds himself, after several days journey, in the Wood beyond the World.

He encounters the Dwarf, who gives him food, and later the Maid, with whom he speaks at length. She warns him of her mistress, who is tired of her current lover (the King's Son) and no doubt has sent the visions to Walter to lure him to her. They plight their love to one another, but Walter cannot touch the Maid, because her mistress' uncanny perception would be sure to detect it.

Continuing to the Lady's "goodly house," Walter finally confronts the ruler of this world. At first disdainful, she eventually takes him as a lover, allowing the King's Son to pursue the Maid. Taking advantage of the dwarf, who spies on her, the Maid proposes a tryst with Walter, then invites the King's Son to her bed and casts a spell over him so that he appears to be the sleeping Walter. The Lady stabs him and in a fit of grief takes her own life. Walter and the Maid flee, pursued by the Dwarf, whom Walter kills.

Their way from the Wood lies through the country of the Bears, who worship the Lady and are accustomed to sacrifice strangers to her. The Maid announces the Lady's death and by means of her own magic convinces them that she herself is the new incarnation of their god. Walter and the Maid continue their journey and, in coming down out of the mountains, are met by a party of armed men who lead them in silence to their city. Stripped naked, Walter is offered his choice of clothes—the rich garments of peace or the battle-stained array of war. He chooses the second and is made King of Stark Wall. Taking the Maid as his Queen, he reigns long and well.

With *The Wood beyond the World*, Morris became increasingly realistic in his treatment of sexuality. Love at first sight is frankly physical. Lust is the first stage in passion. More to the point, Walter's liaison with the Lady—much less the fact of his first marriage—in no way obstructs his union with the Maid. He is neither constrained by Hallblithe's relentless monogamy nor by the spiritual guilt experienced by that other Walter whom Morris portrayed in *The Hill of Venus*, whose intercourse with a figure comparable to the Lady leaves him unalterably devastated. The shared name is more than coincidence. The second Walter reverses the fate of the first. On the other hand, the earlier Walter's fate is mirrored in the old man who refuses to speak about his experiences beyond the mountains. "Clad mostly in the skins of beasts" (XVII, 14), he suggests the archetype of the wild man, which Morris will employ in the later romances as an alternative to the hero's successful integration with society.

Doubtless, *The Wood beyond the World* has an autobiographical component. Jane Morris appears in two roles: the unfaithful wife Walter *can* desert—although he leaves it to his father to actually throw her out of the house—and the Lady whose sexual dominance the Maid enables him to escape. The replacement of the suppressor father in *The Glittering Plain* with the suppressor witch in *The Wood beyond the World* is an important clarification. It is not a strong father who stands in the way of Morris' libido, but the "tall and stately" Pre-Raphaelite beauty he made the mistake of taking for a wife. (Instead of a King's Daughter, there is a King's Son, whose relationship with the Lady has encouraged a brutal selfishness that is the masculine counterpart of the feminine passivity of the King's Daughter.)

What Morris seems to have learned from his marriage was that the women he found sexually attractive were dangerous. Jane's profile was a force at odds with his creative life. Nevertheless, if she is to function as an object of desire, she must participate in the magic of her mistress. Thus she must at once possess supernatural power and cancel its threat to the hero. The problem with the King's Daughter in *The Glittering Plain* was that there was no way for her to free herself from the taint of her father's kingdom. The Maid, too, is tainted, although the exact nature of her power is deliberately unclear. The Lady does not dare kill her, and the Dwarf has learned to fear and despise " 'the Wretch and the Thing.' " " 'Thou fool,' " he tells Walter, " 'wilt think It fair if thou fallest into Its hands, and wilt repent it thereafter, as I did' " (XVII, 28–29). Moreover, this power—whatever its source—is necessary for Walter's escape. " 'Whereas thou speakest of delivering me,' " she tells him at their first meeting, " 'it is more like that I shall deliver thee' " (XVII, 35). Her shape-changing enables them to flee the Wood. Her ability to rejuvenate the flowers with which she had adorned herself enables them to escape the Bears. Yet Morris is careful to distinguish her magic from that of the Lady and to end it with the Maid's loss of physical virginity.

Both Maid and Lady are associated with the power of the natural world—and thus represent a logical development of the figure of Ellen in *News from Nowhere*. The Maid announces herself to the Bears as " 'the very heart of the year's increase,' " explaining " 'that the going of my feet over your pastures shall make them to thrive, both this year and the coming years' " (XVII, 108). But the Maid who brings flowers back to life and sends the drought-stricken Bears a healthy thunder storm is not limited to magic. As Walter's Queen, she returns once more to the Bears, bringing with her a group of husbandmen she has bought from thralldom. Instructing the Bears to accept these visitors and learn their arts, she performs the historical function of elevating them from savagery to barbarism. Furthermore, if offering human sacrifice to the powers of nature is taken as the ultimate symbol of man's abasement to the natural world, then by directing the Bears to give up this practice, she leads them from subservience to into "reasonable strife with Nature." The Maid is thus best described as the means by which a relationship is established and controlled between man and the potency of the natural world.

Her autobiographical narrative is a collection of half-remembered fragments that suggest Morris has not entirely worked out the early stages of the paradigm she exemplifies. However, one episode stands out clearly: " 'I am set to tasks that I would not do, by them that are unwiser than I; and smitten I am by them that are less valiant than I; and I know lack, and stripes, and divers misery. But . . . amongst all these unfriends is a friend to me; an old woman, who telleth me sweet tales of other life, wherein all is high and goodly, or at the least valiant and doughty, and she setteth hope in my heart and learneth me, and maketh me to know much . . . O much . . . so that at last I am grown wise, and wise to be mighty if I durst' " (XVII, 86). Ellen's "magic" is thus given a source in tradition—and a human context. Moreover, it is "the wisdom of a wise maid, and not of a woman" (XVII, 89). Furthermore, if she is to lead them to safety, Walter must forbear her body until they are safe at Stark Wall. And there, their love consummated, she becomes an adoring wife, submissive to her master's power and will.

This transformation is the unresolved problem with the romance. Walter gets off too easily. He has the Maid's magic when he needs it, and it conveniently disappears when it would become a social liability. At worst, he is separated from her for three nights in the mountains after they leave the Bears. This otherwise gratuitous episode seems to have been meant to emphasize his vulnerability without her. But his crowning at Stark Wall cancels the message. And when she humbles herself before the new-made King, the reversal is complete.

And yet in other terms this conclusion marks an important revaluation of the hero's quest. Unlike Guest in *News from Nowhere*, whose quest takes him to the Oxfordshire haymaking, or Hallblithe, who returns to the pastoral setting of Cleveland by the Sea, Walter makes his final home in a city. For once Morris seems willing to accept urban life as a symbol of social integration. But Walter and the Maid are not merely adopted by an established society. The king-making of Stark Wall echoes the ceremonial reaffirmation of tribal origins Morris granted the Burgdalers in *The Roots of the Mountains*. When the royal bloodline falls, the people of Stark Wall send men to the mountain pass from which they believe their primitive ancestors once came. Walter is thus an embodiment of the energies and virtues of gens society. Having successfully confronted nature in the wild, he is able to renew civilization with a dose of its power. Hallblithe, one senses, will live out his days in Cleveland by the Sea much as he would have if he had never visited the Glittering Plain. Walter's fate, on the other hand, is a direct consequence of his quest. He is thus more satisfactory both as a character in his own romance and as an archetypal figure susceptible to development in the closely related romances that follow fast upon *The Wood beyond the World*.

III   The Well at the World's End *(1896)*

A year after *The Wood beyond the World*, the Kelmscott Press issued the first edition of *Child Christopher and Goldilind the Fair* (1895). Based on the lay of Havelock the Dane, the tale lacks the imaginative freedom of Morris' original romances; however, its treatment of common themes and figures confirms their importance in his later work. The symmetrical plot involves the restoration of an orphaned prince and princess to the thrones from which they were excluded by unfaithful guardians. Its virgin heroine is imprisoned by a sinister old woman—and four other virgins undergo a similar fate in a subplot! Both hero and heroine flee from their captors into the wild, where both seem to partake of the potency of the natural world. The telling gesture of Goldilind's emancipation is a forest baptism (XVII, 174), after which she encounters Christopher wearing "a garland of white may blossom" (XVII, 177). The hero asserts his manhood and thus wins his father's kingdom by overthrowing an older, battle-experienced adversary in single combat. Christopher's best friend falls in love with Goldilind and takes to wandering in the wide world, but after many years he returns and together all live happily ever after.

These archetypes—baptism in nature, the enslaved virgin, the older, rival male, the rival brother—all play roles in *The Well at the World's End*. Longest of the prose romances, it was also the longest in being written. (Morris called it "The Interminable.") Begun early in 1892, it was not completed until 1894 and not published until 1896—although sections had been typeset as early as 1892. Its chronological relationship to *The Wood beyond the World* is thus somewhat confused, and its leisurely exposition difficult to summarize.

Ralph, youngest of the four sons of the "kinglet" of Upmeads, disobeys his parents and sets forth "to see the ways of other men, and to strive for life" (XVIII, 1). To aid him in his quest, his "gossip" (godmother) Dame Katherine gives him "a little necklace of gold and green and blue stones," enjoining him to " 'wear this around thy neck, and let no man take it from thee, and I think it will be salvation to thee in peril, and good luck to thee in the time of questing; so that it shall be to thee as if thou hadst drunk of the WELL AT THE WORLD'S END' " (XVIII, 11). The meaning of her words remains unspecified, but when Ralph stops for lunch in the village of Bourton Abbas the maiden who waits on him warns him of the Wood Perilous, in which her lover has recently disappeared, and expresses her yearning to " 'drink a draught from the WELL AT THE WORLD'S END' " (XVIII, 40). He goes his way, but before he sets forth, she and Ralph kiss one another passionately.

In the Wood, Ralph rescues a woman being led in bondage by the men of the Burg of the Four Friths. She, in turn, enables Ralph to escape the Burg, along with Roger of the Ropewalk, who has attached himself to Ralph as a servant, and four men of the Fellowship of the Dry Tree, whom the Burgers had intended to hang. She is the Lady of Abundance, and Roger takes Ralph to the Castle of Abundance, where he awaits her coming. He at length finds her, but is overcome by the Knight of the Sun, her husband. At the Lady's plea, his life is spared, and by her means the two escape, pausing in their flight to make love in the midst of the forest. She has drunk of the Well at the World's End and promises to go there once again with Ralph. But that evening the Knight of the Sun comes upon them, slays the Lady, and is himself slain by Ralph.

Ralph eventually falls in with his brother Blaise, who has become a prosperous merchant, and, later, with Clement Chapman (Dame Katherine's husband). In his deep sense of loss, he yearns for the Well, and dreams of the maiden from Bourton Abbas, who identifies herself as " 'a sending of the woman whom thou hast loved' " and urges him to " 'go seek the Well at the World's End not all alone: and the seeker may find me: and whereas thou wouldst know my name, I hight Dorothea' " (XVIII, 220).

Following rumors of the whereabouts of the Well, Ralph joins Clement, with whom he journeys as far as the city of Goldburg. On route, he finds evidence that "Dorothea" has taken the same path and been captured, probably to be sold as a thrall. Here, too, he acquires a thrall of his own: Bull Shockhead, a mountain tribesman he subdues in combat. Ralph is lured from Goldburg by a eunuch minstrel, who promises to take him in safety to Utterbol, where "Dorothea" has apparently been taken. He is intended as a lover for the Lady of Utterbol, whose husband has siezed "Dorothea." Ralph is taken prisoner, but eventually escapes and comes upon the maiden of Bourton Abbas, who has on her own escaped Utterbol. Together they meet the Sage of Swevenham, "a friend of the Well" who teaches them the lore they need to undertake its quest.

It is a weakness of the romance that from this (its approximate midpoint) the narrative offers little doubt about the ultimate fates of hero and heroine. Ralph and Ursula (her real name) cross a volcanic mountain range (another reminiscence of Iceland), winter in a cave, and the following spring are met by emissaries of the Innocent Folk, who marry the pair and lead them through their land to the House of the Sorceress (where the Lady of Abundance spent her childhood). From there, the two lovers—now husband and wife—set off alone. They cross a great waste and come upon the Dry Tree, where Ursula saves Ralph from succumbing to despair. Continuing, they at length reach the Well, which flows from rocks at the edge of the sea, and drink of its waters.

Their quest accomplished, Ralph and Ursula return to civilization, joined by the Sage of Swevenham, who realizes that he has wasted his powers living as a hermit. As they retrace Ralph's journey from Upmeads, they either find wrong righted or right wrong themselves.

Bull Shockhead has avenged his brother by killing the Lord of Utterbol; wedding the Lady of Utterbol, he has become a beneficent ruler for the hitherto tyrant-ridden land. Similarly, the wicked overlords of the Burg of the Four Friths have been overthrown. Ralph and Ursula eventually reach Upmeads in time to save it from invasion. His father steps down and names Ralph king, and, with the strength and longevity they won from the Well, Ralph and Ursula rule long and prosperously.

In overall pattern, *The Well at the World's End* parallels *The Roots of the Mountains*. Like Face-of-God, Ralph leaves his family, encounters a woman—or two—in the wild, through whom he gains the power and wisdom necessary to return to his home and save it from an external foe. Yet Ralph's heroism is suspiciously easy. He is a "lucky" man with whom all women fall in love. Both Ursula and the Lady of Abundance love him at first sight. The Queen of Goldburg deserts her throne when he refuses her. The Lady of Utterbol is similarly entranced. Only at two points in the narrative is Ralph really vulnerable: when he is defeated by the Knight of the Sun and when he starts to drink the poisonous water at the Dry Tree. In both instances, he is saved by a woman. The Lady of Abundance rescues him from her husband; Ursula breaks the spell of the Tree. Even his quest is initiated by a woman. Without Dame Katherine's gift, he would not—presumably—have reached the Well.

Ralph's passivity and the corresponding strength of the Lady and Ursula argue that it is no longer the hero, but the heroine who has come to dominate Morris' imagination. This new perspective was evident in *The Wood beyond the World*, but the Maid's loss of power with virginity was an evasion of the full implications of her role and the Lady's unalloyed wickedness ignored the ambivalence of her potency. In *The Well at the World's End*, Morris attempts to resolve these problems by presenting the heroine in three guises: Sorceress, Lady, and Maid. Through the first, Morris explores the negative implications of the archetype; through the second, its ambivalence; through the third, he attempts to reduce it to manageable scale. Ralph only directly encounters the second and third versions of the figure. Moreover, it is not their power but their weakness that rouses his passion. He encounters both in situations of bondage or attack.[3] The Lady is captive when he first meets her; Ursula is dominated by her brutish brother, and later she is imprisoned by the matriarch at Hampton under Scaur (from whom she is rescued by the Lady) and by the Lord of Utterbol. Significantly, she withholds herself from Ralph while they winter in "The Vale of Sweet Chestnuts," until she is attacked—appropriately—by a bear. Rescuing her, Ralph kisses her so "greedily" that she fears the " 'sweet season' " is " 'somewhat marred by our desire' " (XIX, 54).

But it is the Lady, not Ursula, who undergoes the greater bondage, and her autobiographical narrative is the central event of the romance. Interestingly enough, she tells her story to Ralph immediately after "between them in the wilderness was all the joy of love that might be." It is thus his compensation for the loss of virginity: through sexual union he assumes her knowledge and is thus spared the need to undergo the extremes of treachery and violence that have characterized her life.

She has drunk of the Well at the World's End, but beauty, power, and long life have earned her a sinister reputation, and where she has most loved she has brought greatest destruction. In contrast to the hero, who must forcibly wrest himself from father and mother, she never knows her parents or lineage. Her first memory is of the House of the Sorceress, for whom as a child she tended goats and spun yarn. The Sorceress practices a form of natural magic, the most notable achievement of which is technological: while she sits naked, singing from a book of lore, her cloth is woven by itself. (What she does with all this fabric is uncertain.)

Apparently the girl is intended as a lure for seekers of the Well. And apparently her innocence is a factor in this intention. When she discovers the secret of her mistress' "weaving," the Sorceress threatens her with death, but instead sacrifices the girl's pet goat on a stone altar and smears them both with its blood. Despite these precautions, education and sexual awakening render the girl unfit for the Sorceress' purposes. And both follow from an act of immersion in nature:

> "On a day of May-tide I fared abroad with my goats, and went far with them, further from the house than I had been as yet. The day was the fairest of the year, and I rejoiced in it, and felt as if some exceeding great good were about to befall me. . . . So I went till I came to a little flowery dell, beset with blossoming whitethorns and with a fair stream running through it; . . . And the sun was hot about noontide, so I did off my raiment, which was rough and poor, and more meet for winter than May-tide, and I entered a pool of the clear water, and bathed me and sported therein, smelling the sweet scent of the whitethorns and harkening to the song of the many birds; and when I came forth from the water, the air was so soft and sweet to me, and the flowery grass so kind to my feet, and the May-blooms fell upon my shoulders,

that I was loth to do on my rough raiment hastily, and withal I looked to see no child of man in that wilderness: so I sported myself there a long while, and milked a goat and drank of the milk, and crowned myself with whitethorn and hare-bells; and held the blossoms in my hand, and felt that I also had some might in me, and that I should not be a thrall of that sorceress for ever." (XVIII, 156)

The Sorceress' power derives from human sacrifice to nature; her "technology" is gained at the cost of alienation from the natural processes she attempts to control. Her thrall, on the other hand, becomes strong through participation in these very processes. In keeping with the season, she casts off her winter rags. Naked, she does not merely intensify her perception of nature; she becomes a living component of the landscape. As if summoned by the girl's gesture, an " 'old woman grey haired . . . but with shining bright eyes' " appears coming down the hillside. On this and subsequent days she teaches the girl "letters" and knowledge " 'of the world which I had not yet seen, of its fairness and its foulness; of life and death, and desire and disappointment, and despair; so that when she had done, if I were wiser than erst, I was perchance little more joyous; and yet I said to myself that come what would I would be a part of all that' " (XVIII, 158).

The days pass. Then, on Midsummer Day, when the girl goes to "the Dale of Lore" she meets, instead of the wise woman, a handsome knight " 'in bright shining armour with a gay surcoat of green embroidered with flowers over it' " (XVIII, 160). They speak for a while; he starts to leave, but returns to her; " 'and there in that place, in a little while, we loved each other sorely' " (XVIII, 161). As a token of their meeting, he gives her a necklace like Ralph's, then departs. The wise woman comes and gives her a gift to go along with the necklace—a sharp knife. The girl returns to her mistress, who, seeing the necklace, falls upon her with " 'a dreadful screaming roar,' " but the girl is ready and stabs her attacker in the breast.

Freed of her mistress, the girl wanders in the world and is eventually reunited with the knight, who takes her with him to his father's kingdom. But the king rejects her and plots her death. They attempt to flee, but are captured and the girl is nearly burnt as a witch. A long civil war ensues. At length, on his father's death, the knight is made king and his wife—now "the Lady"—takes her place beside him on the throne. Still, she—not the old king—is blamed by many for the years of internecine strife. And so when her husband dies, she is once again in danger. The old woman reappears and together they travel to drink of the Well. Rejuvenated and powerful, the Lady becomes patroness of the Robin-Hood Fellowship of the Dry Tree, now in bitter struggle with the Burg of the Four Friths, and, apparently against her will, wife of the Knight of the Sun.

As she killed herself standing over what she took to be the slain body of Golden Walter, the Lady in *The Wood Beyond the World* cried out " 'I shall forget; I shall forget; and the new days shall come.' Then was there silence of her a little, and thereafter she cried out in a terrible voice: 'O no, no, no! I cannot forget: I cannot forget' (XVII, 93). Only in that moment did Morris come close to recognizing the tragic self-destructiveness of her power. The Lady of Abundance, who embodies attributes of both the Lady and the Maid in the earlier romance, develops this tragedy in significant detail. Like Ralph, she is irresistably attractive. But for her this is more a liability than an asset. Forced to reject her suitors, many of them become enemies whose lies and treachery again and again threaten her life. Without a home and lineage, she is perennially vulnerable. Her identity itself is in question. For many she is a witch. Waiting for her in the Castle of Abundance, even Ralph wonders if "this woman on whom he had set his heart was herself no real woman but a devil, and one of the goddesses of the ancient world, and his heart was sore and troubled by many doubts and hopes and fears" (XVIII, 104). In the Land of Abundance, she is very nearly worshipped as a "goddess of the ancient world," but she is too strong to live within its narrow geographic and intellectual confines. Thus, the one place in which she is fully welcomed is inadequate to her desires. On the other hand, when she finally finds a man who is her equal, they are divided (through her death) by the vestiges of her past life.

The Lady herself doubts her fitness for Ralph. Having rescued Ursula from prison at Hampton under Scaur, she " 'went with her into the wildwood, and taught her wisdom of the way [to the Well] and what she was to do. . . . she was so sweet and yet with a kind of pith in her both of soul and body, and wise withal and quiet, that I feared her, though I loved her; yea and still do: for I deem her better than me, and meeter for thee and thy love than I be' " (XVIII, 195). She thus performs for Ursula the same service the wise woman performed for her. Significantly, although the Lady appears to be able to send Ralph his dream of Ursula, she lacks the power to give her her right name. Ursula, on the other hand, *is* able to assume the Lady's role as patroness of the Dry Tree and mistress of the Land of

Abundance. But if Ursula's purely "natural" power saves Ralph from the "supernatural" potency of the Lady—who, despite their initial encounter, remains the dominant partner—Morris is careful to keep this substitution from coming about too easily. The loss of the Lady is a shock from which Ralph never fully recovers. When he and Ursula come, as man and wife, to the House of the Sorceress, he breaks down in tears. And later, when an old friend congratulates him on having " 'wedded into the World of living men, and not to a dream of the land of Fairy,' " the comparison " 'woundeth my heart' " (XIX, 137). There was an intensity in his first, brief experience of love he can never recapture. And it is precisely this loss that initiates his quest for the Well at the World's End.

Upmeads, and the lands surrounding it, are Christian kingdoms. To reach the Well, Ralph must first travel through pagan territories, where the rules of chivalry are less and less honored, and then, by way of the primitive society of the Innocent Folk, cross the wilderness itself. He must, in other words, regress in time through earlier stages of human culture to the antecedents of culture. The Well, placed at the World's End, is thus a symbol for the origins of human life. Having drunk of its water, "it seemed to them that they had come into the very Garden of God" (XIX, 87). But its setting prevents us from identifying the Well with a Judeo-Christian Eden. Despite their "Saracen" beads and various quasi-religious rituals Ralph and Ursula must undergo in their quest, its goal is purely natural. In the words of the Lady, " 'in the Well at the World's End is no evil, but only the Quenching of Sorrow, and Clearing of the Eyes that they may behold' " (XVIII, 168). It quenches sorrow by renewing the drinker's participation in the natural life of the earth; it clears his eyes by offering a purely naturalistic explanation of human potency. This meaning is borne out by two inscriptions: above the well is written, "YE WHO HAVE COME A LONG WAY TO LOOK UPON ME, DRINK OF ME, IF YE DEEM THAT YE BE STRONG ENOUGH IN DESIRE TO BEAR LENGTH OF DAYS: OR ELSE DRINK NOT; BUT TELL YOUR FRIENDS AND THE KINDREDS OF THE EARTH HOW YE HAVE SEEN A GREAT MARVEL"; and on the rim of the golden cup from which they drink runs a similar warning, " 'THE STRONG OF HEART SHALL DRINK FROM ME' " (XIX, 81–82). The power of the Well is a function of human desire. Strength of life is only fitting for men and women who accept life itself as sufficient to their desires. In the words of the Sage of Swevenham, " 'if ye love not the earth and the world with all your souls, and will not strive all ye may to be frank and happy therein, your toil and peril aforesaid shall win you no blessing, but a curse' " (XIX, 36).

And yet the quest for the Well turns on a paradox. If one is content with the earth, then one accepts its laws of natural process and limitation. Only those who reject the merely natural undertake the quest to begin with. The pattern of the successful quest is thus dialectic of rejection and rediscovery closely related to high romantic paradigms of individual development. The dessicated bodies Ralph and Ursula pass on their journey across the wilderness and find clustered around the Dry Tree are ample evidence that many, probably most, other questers are incapable of this dialectic. What they find in their attempt to master nature is merely nature in its most hostile form, or, if they get that far, the poisonous waters at the foot of the Dry Tree—the image of sterile selfhood Morris offers as an antithesis to the Well.

Ursula's love saves Ralph from succumbing to the lure of the Dry Tree. Like Pharamond in *Love is Enough,* he is "freed" from bondage to a selfish goal—whether strength or forgetfulness—by his own liberated eros. But the failed questers at the Dry Tree are only one alternative to Ralph and Ursula's quest. In a key passage, the Elder of the Innocent Folk contrasts his people's philosophy of life with Ralph's:

"our folk live well and hale, and without the sickness and pestilence, such as I have heard oft befall folk in other lands. . . . Of strife and war also we know naught: nor do we desire aught which we may not easily attain to. Therefore we live long, and we fear the Gods if we should strive to live longer, lest they should bring upon us war and sickness, and overweening desire, and weariness of life. Moreover it is little like that all of us should seek to the Well at the World's End; and those few that sought and drank should be stronger and wiser than the others, and should make themselves earthly gods, and, maybe, should torment the others of us and make their lives a very burden to be borne. . . . But for you, guests, it is otherwise, for ye of the World beyond the Mountains are stronger and more godlike than we, as all tales tell; and ye wear away your lives desiring that which ye may scarce get. . . . Therefore ye know sickness and sorrow, and oft ye die before your time, so that ye must depart and leave undone things which ye deem ye were born to do; which to all men is grievous. And because of all this ye desire healing and thriving, whether good come of it, or ill. Therefore ye do but right to seek to the Well at the World's End, that ye may the better accomplish that which behoveth you, and that ye may serve your fellows and deliver them from the thralldom of those that be strong and unwise and unkind, of whom we have heard strange tales." (XIX, 65–66)

Ralph "reddens," and Ursula hastily changes the subject: yet the perspective of the Innocent Folk has become an inescapable qualification of their quest.

On the other hand, the pastoral existence of the Innocent Folk is never an alternative for Ralph and Ursula. Their way of life is predicated on an ignorance of the outside world Ralph and Ursula have long ago forfeited. Moreover, Morris' anthropological treatment of primitive society reminds us that it cannot be taken as a utopian vision.

The real alternatives to Ralph's quest lie back on the other side of the mountains, in the world of experience to which he must inevitably return. From the start he is faced with the need to make choices. The monks at Hingham-on-the-Way (his first stop) try to enlist him in their army; the Burgers of the Four Friths offer him a similar opportunity; his brother Blaise attempts to secure his services for the merchant city in which he has come to power; the Queen of Goldburg would have him as her king. Priests, warriors, merchants, and potentates all seek to draw him into their classes. And even among the "friends of the Well" there are alternatives to his choice. The "Wise Woman of Sarras," who taught the Lady in the Dale of Lore—and also gave Ralph's "gossip" the beads she in turn gave to him—elected to seek wisdom; the Sage of Swevenham also elected wisdom, but chose for many years to hold it from the world. On the other hand, the King who built Goldburg chose, like Ralph, an active life, but wasted his powers in vainglory.

Ralph's journey is thus at once a quest for the potency (and healing strength) of the natural world and a quest for his own vocation. And yet there is never any doubt as to his ultimate decision. He grows through his experience, but his identity itself remains stable, and he rejects the alternatives without testing them through any significant commitment of time or energy. Thus, just as the Lady of Abundance saved him from the bitterest encounters with experience, it is Ursula who takes on the burden of profound individuation. Unlike Ralph, she reaches the Well without supernatural aid. (She, too, has a necklace, given her by the Lady of Abundance, but it is only talismanic when given by one of the opposite sex.) It is she who risks most; it is she who seeks and finds an identity that was at best latent in her early life. It was inevitable, then, that Morris' next romance should focus on the active heroine rather than the relatively passive hero.

IV   The Water of the Wondrous Isles *(1897)*

Birdalone's early history is yet another version of the captive virgin archetype. Stolen from her mother as an infant, she is raised by a witch at her farmstead in a clearing between the vast inland "Water" and the ill-omened forest of Evilshaw. Like the Lady of Abundance, her coming of age is effected through the intervention of a foster-mother, who teaches her wisdom and encourages her to flee her captor. But the precise nature of this figure is given a further refinement. In keeping with the paradigm, their meeting is preceded by a scene in which Birdalone undresses herself in the summer forest and sits sewing in the shade of an oak tree, "that she might feel all the pleasure of the cool shadow and what air was stirring, and the kindness of the greensward upon her very body" (XX, 15). Suddenly, she sees "standing before her the shape of a young woman as naked as herself, save that she had an oak wreath round about her loins." The newcomer is Habundia, a wood spirit "not of the children of Adam" who appears now and subsequently as Birdalone's double. Her name, like that of the Lady of Abundance, suggests the abundance of the natural world, here identified specifically with the forest. It is through her reflection in nature, then, that Birdalone becomes aware of her own identity and consequently is able to assert herself against the witch.

The witch, interestingly enough, is not at home in the forest. To pass through it, she must alter her appearance. Like that of the sorceress in *The Well at the World's End,* her power over nature is gained at the cost of alienation from the natural world. Its prime achievement is the "Boat of Sending." Its stem and stern smeared with her blood, this boat takes "the sender" to the destiny of her will. Supernatural power is thus explicitly a function of human blood sacrifice. Moreover, the source of that power is also explicit: At the death of the witch-wife, the boat breaks up and "a big serpent, mouldy and hairy, grey and brown-flecked, came forth from under the stem and went into the water and up the bank and so into the dusk of the alder-wood" (XX, 320).

Birdalone's power is also derived from the natural world. But it is

156   WILLIAM MORRIS

not gained through an attempt to dominate nature. Moreover, there are strict limits to her dependence on Habundia. Preparing to flee the witch-wife, she rejects Habundia's counsel of secrecy, " 'lest I become a guileful woman, with nought good in me save the fairness of my body.' " Significantly, her flight is precipitated by her loss of Habundia's ring. Taking the Boat of Sending, she escapes the witch, only to find herself naked and powerless at the castle of the witch's equally malevolent sister on the Island of Increase Unsought.

But before she is taken before the Mistress of the Island, she encounters her three thralls, Aurea, Viridis, and Atra, who promise to do what they can to aid her, relying on their mistress' one weakness: she can seldom remember anything if it is out of her sight for twenty-four hours—which is to say, her power entails the loss of the temporal component of her identity. Their strategy works. Birdalone in recompense is asked to bring tokens to the lovers of the women—Baudoin (the Golden Knight), Hugh (the Green Knight), and Arthur (the Black Squire)—from whom they were stolen.

Birdalone once more embarks in the Boat of Sending, which takes her to four more islands: The Isle of the Young and the Old, the Isle of Queens, the Isle of Kings, and the Isle of Nothing. All four are symbolic of the sterility brought about by the two witches' dominance over the Water. At length, she reaches "The Castle of the Quest," where the three Champions have stationed themselves in their quest for their three ladies. On Birdalone's counsel, they take the Boat of Sending and leave her in the care of the castellan.

Drawn by an irresistible urge to visit the Valley of Greywethers, Birdalone connives to steal from the castle the morning of the very day the three knights return with their ladies. Rescuing her, Baudoin is slain and it becomes clear that Arthur has transferred his love from Atra to Birdalone, who returns it, but feels bound to respect Atra's prior claim—particularly since it was Atra who played the chief role in saving her from the witch's sister. Taking advantage of the knights' absence, Birdalone leaves the Castle. She hires an old man and his two sons (Gerard, Robert, and Giles) to accompany her and eventually makes her way to the City of the Five Crafts. Here she is reunited with her long-lost mother and together they make a good living with their remarkable—apparently congenital—skill at embroidery. But when her mother dies, Birdalone is moved to seek Arthur. Leaving Gerard and his sons, she returns to the Castle of the Quest, only to find it deserted and Arthur's whereabouts uncertain. Once more she embarks on the Boat of Sending, which takes her, by way of the other Wondrous Isles to the Isle of Increase Unsought. Everywhere she lands all has changed. Life—and sexual desire—has returned to the first four islands, but the fifth, formerly an earthly paradise, is now a barren waste.

However, when she seeks to return to the Boat of Sending, it has disappeared. Calling on her Woodmother for help, Birdalone plunges into the Water, intending to swim as far as her strength will take her. On the point of exhaustion, she comes upon a floating tree, which bears her to shore at the witch-wife's cottage.

Her mistress is dead, but Habundia is waiting for her in the forest. Birdalone tells her her story, and Habundia promises to help her. Arthur's desolation has driven him to madness, and he is living in Evilshaw as a wild man. Through Habundia's aid, he is restored to his senses and united with Birdalone. To further their happiness, Habundia arranges for Hugh, Atra, Aurea, and Viridis to join them in the forest. Ultimately, the party agree to live together in Utterhay (the town from which Birdalone was originally stolen), along with Gerard and his sons, one of whom later marries Aurea. Hugh and Arthur become war dukes of the city, and together they live in happiness, regularly visiting Habundia in Evilshaw.

The striking aspect of this plot is the frequency with which Birdalone must run away and begin her life anew. She escapes from the witch-wife; she twice flees her friends at the Castle of the Quest; she forsakes the Five Crafts. Although she has the irresistable good looks Morris bestows on his heroes and heroines, her life is far from "lucky." Indeed, her experiences lead finally to an attempted suicide, from which she is saved by Habundia (who sends the floating tree to her aid). And her final encounter with the witch-wife, whom she believes alive, suggests the failure of her quest for individuation: " 'Dame, I am come back unto thee, as thou seest, in even such plight as I fled from thee; and I have a mind to dwell in this land: what sayest thou?' " (XX, 316). There is a Wordsworthian flavor in her return to the natural setting of her childhood, where Habundia appears as a younger Birdalone, unscathed by experience, to heal the psychic wounds she has endured and prepare her for reunion with Arthur.

The reunion takes place, yet, in contrast with the simple poetic justice of the earlier romances, *The Water of the Wondrous Isles* stresses the cost of individual success. Birdalone escapes the fate of the Lady of Abundance—with whom she has so much in common— but only because she deliberately thwarts her own sexuality. Moreover, her happiness depends, inescapably, on the unhappiness of another woman. Arthur, like Golden Walter and Ralph of Up-meads, loves one woman before he comes to love another. But Atra neither proves unfaithful nor is murdered by a jealous rival. And her presence in the closing chapters of the romance qualifies the happiness of hero and heroine.

When Birdalone tells Habundia of her three friends, the Wood-mother is particularly interested in Viridis, whose green costume suggests a special relationship with the natural. But in the end it is Atra, not Viridis, who captures her sympathy. Like Habundia, Atra is wise. But her black habiliments signify a wisdom derived from human suffering rather than natural lore. She is thus Habundia's complement—a relationship both appear to recognize and enjoy. Together, they represent the two sides of Birdalone's personality—tragic self-awareness and healthy "animal" happiness—neither of which separately is an adequate model for the full development of her personality.

Birdalone's life evolves dialectically between these polarities. Alienated from nature, the witch-wife is a crude prototype of Atra (whose black is the traditional color of witches' garments), from whom Birdalone instinctively rebels. Yet Habundia, who fosters her rebel-lion, must in turn be rejected, for even the Woodmother acknowl-edges " 'there is something in thine heart which we, who are not children of Adam, may not understand.' " Yet Birdalone's sub-sequent life at the Castle of the Quest—the image of heroic achieve-ment Morris sets against her earlier life in the forest—is also a form of captivity. She is uncomfortable in the role of "weak" female into which she is forced by the three Champions and their castellan. Her fascination with the Valley of the Greywethers is partially a magic spell woven by the Red Knight (the enemy of the Champions, who seeks to capture Birdalone), but it is also a reflex from the indoor world of the Castle. Hence, her exclamation at the first sight of the mountains ringing the valley: " 'Oh! but thou art beautiful, O earth, thou art beautiful!' " But Greywethers turns out to be a false nature—a hostile world of stone, rather than one of leaf and flower—and her attempt to participate in its potency results in Baudoin's needless death.

Consequently, her second flight from the Castle of the Quest is not a return to nature, but an acceptance of human tragedy. Interestingly enough, her means of escape is plying a craft in a city of craftsmen. Like Morris himself, Birdalone seems to have gained emotional solace from working with her hands. And, like his own wallpapers and fabrics, the subjects of her embroidery are invariably naturalistic. Thus, the imagery of her work is a means of recapturing the vitality of her childhood in the forest: an attempt through art to synthesize the two elements in her personality.

The attempt works, but only for a while. Eventually, repressed desire reasserts itself and Birdalone leaves the Five Crafts in search of Arthur. However, it is not easy to find him. Her route, which starts as a simple return to the Castle of the Quest, becomes a retracing of her life to the scene of childhood innocence, which she must rediscover if she is to complete herself as an adult. Thus Habundia is not merely a stage in her growing up, but a necessary component of Birdalone's mature happiness. And because she is necessary, Morris carefully underlines the limitations to her power. She is a creature of the forest who cannot adapt herself to human civilization. Even entering the witch-wife's cottage to share a meal with Birdalone causes her to shrink in size—until Birdalone kisses her and restores her form. More important, she is incapable of full sympathy for human suffering. As Birdalone tearfully tells her "the tale of her love for Arthur . . . the Woodmother was ever as sweet and kind unto her as could be; yet might another than a lover have seen that much of this was strange unto her, and she looked upon Birdalone as a child who has broken a toy, and is hard to comfort for the loss of it, though there be a many more in the world" (XX, 326–27).

By making his heroine the central figure of the romance, Morris subordinates Arthur to peripheral importance. However, his passivity is not merely an effect of this shift in perspective. Like Birdalone's active struggle to come to terms with her own fate, Arthur's passive acceptance of necessity is thematic to the romance. This is most evident in his encounter with the witch-wife's sister on the Isle of Increase Unsought. Aware that the three Champions are on the way, she gives her thralls a potion to make them invisible. Then, she allows the knights to search the island for their loves, while she turns her charms on Arthur. At length, as he sees it, their only chance lies in his " 'bedding her.' " His sacrifice is of some avail, but they are still unable to find the ladies. In time, the witch tires of Arthur and turns to Hugh, who refuses her and so doing discovers the secret of her power, which thus enables them to fulfill their quest. Accordingly, it is not clear that Arthur's sexual sacrifice is necessary. (If, like Hugh, he had rejected the witch, they might have discovered her secret all the sooner.) His gesture can thus be interpreted as an attempt to exorcise the guilt he feels for having fallen in love with Birdalone.

Similarly, when Birdalone flees the Castle of the Quest for the second time, he does not follow what one might take to be his natural impulse to search for her. Instead, he tries to control his feelings by throwing himself into public activity, and, when that fails, by becoming a hermit and later—inevitably—a wild man. All are modes of escape, rather than self-discovery; all fail, because none is a match for his devouring self-consciousness. For Arthur the forest is an alien world, in which left on his own he sinks into bestiality. Approached as a locus for introspection, nature is not a solace but a threat. (It takes Habundia to restore him to his senses, but this comes about as a favor to Birdalone, not though any special concern for Arthur.) Thus in the figure of Arthur, Morris examines the negative implications of his earlier "lucky" heroes. For Arthur, "luck" becomes passivity; self-confidence, a gnawing sense of guilt from which, without the heroine's intervention, he has no means of rescuing himself.

Despite its ritualized patterns of color and number, *The Water of the Wondrous Isles* does not follow a strictly organized design. Unlike *The Well at the World's End,* it lacks an overall structure of journey and return. Granted, there is a return—but it comes as an admission of failure, rather than of triumph. In writing the romance, Morris seems to have become increasingly fascinated by the vulnerability of its heroine and hero. Fittingly, its conclusion is less a resolution than an elaborate compromise between the forces at work in the romance. War dukes of Utterhay, Hugh and Arthur play a powerful role in the city without fully assimilating themselves to its society. Aurea marries, but Atra does not. Nor does she completely overcome her sense of loss. From time to time "would she fall moody and spoken." Then she leaves her friends to spend a month or more with Habundia in the forest, from which she returns "calm and kind and well-liking." But the significant image is Utterhay itself. Habundia cannot enter the city; although its sinister reputation wears somewhat away, the people of Utterhay continue to fear Evilshaw. The city on the edge of the forest is thus an image of the ultimate irreconcilability of the polarities Morris envisioned coming together in the urbanized country life of *News from Nowhere.* Only the few—Birdalone and her companions—can dwell safely in both worlds. And even for them the relationship is not a synthesis but a dialectic.

V   The Sundering Flood *(1897)*

The Sundering Flood, which Morris left nearly complete at the time of his death, is based on a parallel structure that suggests the fundamental equality of hero and heroine. But the greater part of the romance focuses directly on Osberne, and Elfhild's story is presented as an internal narrative—although shorter than it might have been had Morris fully developed the closing chapters. Raised on opposite banks of a mighty river (the Sundering Flood), they fall in love as children, speaking to one another across an impassible barrier. The subsequent episodes of the romance recount the separate journeys and trials through which they are ultimately united and return together to Osberne's family stead (Wethermel).

Like the earlier heroines, Elfhild is associated with natural magic. Before she encounters Osberne she is given gifts by the dwarves—a magic pipe (for calling her sheep) and "a necklace of gold and gems; gold and emerald, gold and sapphire, gold and ruby" (XXI, 36). Later, after she has been stolen by and escaped from raiders, she undertakes her journey in search of Osberne in the company of a foster mother whose magic sees the two women through various dangers. But, what is more noteworthy, Osberne too has a relationship with the powers of the earth. Steelhead—a masculine version of Habundia—gives the boy first a magic bow and arrows, later the sword "Boardcleaver . . . fashioned by the fathers of old" (XXI, 51), and reappears at crucial points in his life to aid or protect him. Osberne thus represents a significant development in Morris' concept of the hero. No longer does he depend on the heroine for his link with the potency of the natural world. No longer is it necessary to diffuse the threatening power of the heroine.

For these reasons, Osberne is Morris' most satisfactory representation of a masculine self-image in the late romances. Like Morris, Osberne is a "natural" poet—and a craftsman as well. Orphaned at an early age and brought up by his grandparents, he effects the rejection of mother and father less completely realized by Morris' other heroes. And his self-characterization as a boy-man in the early chapters of the romance suggests a similar configuration in Morris' identity—his inability to fully conceive of himself as an adult.

But the pattern of Osberne's maturation suggests the very element missing in Morris' own experience: an adequate paternal self-object. The gift of Steelhead's sword—symbolic of initiation into adult masculinity—is accompanied by a ceremony not unlike the parallel awakenings of the Lady of Abundance in *The Well at the World's End* and Birdalone in *The Water of the Wondrous Isles*. As they sit conversing by the bank of "a bright stream," Osberne expresses a wish to " 'take to the water this hot noon' ":

"It is well thought of, lad," said Steelhead, "and that the more, as I must needs see thee naked if I am to strengthen thee as I am minded to do." So they did off their raiment, both of them, and went into the biggest of the pools hard by; and if Steelhead were a noble-looking man clad, far nobler was he to look on naked, for he was both big and well shapen, so that better might not be. (XXI, 52)

Steelhead leaves the water and dresses, then

called the lad to him all naked as he was, and said: "Stand thou before me, youngling, and I will give thee a gift which shall go well with Boardcleaver." And the lad stood still before him, and Steelhead laid his hands on the head of him first, and let them abide there a while; then he passed his hands over the shoulders and arms of the boy, and his legs and thighs and breast, and all over his body; and therewith he said: "In our days and the olden time it was the wont of fathers to bless their children in this wise; but for thee, thy father is dead, and thy nighest kinsman is little-hearted and somewhat of a churl. Thus then have I done to thee to take the place of a father to thee, I who am of the warriors of while agone." (XXI, 52–53)

The ceremony has two parts. Before the laying on of hands can occur, Osberne must first take in the sight of a naked adult male—that is, of his own potential self, perceived in frankly physical terms. Osberne, too, is naked ("lank, yet for his age . . . full well shapen"). What takes place is thus both the discovery of a role model and an acceptance of the boy's narcissistic exhibitionism, which can, in turn, lead to the integration of narcissistic drives in his adult self. (In contrast, Morris' lifelong ambivalence towards his own self-assertiveness suggests his failure to accomplish this integration.)

The second element of the ceremony, the laying on of hands, connects Osberne with an historical tradition of heroic manhood. The gesture seems to derive from Morris' habitual concern with the past. Yet its relation to Osberne's discovery of a surrogate father suggests that this concern may have been Morris' attempt to compensate for his lack of a masculine role model and thus a symptom of the incomplete integration of his self-image. Furthermore, Steelhead's ritual equates history with the human body itself. To affirm historical tradition and to outline the boy's physical lineaments are one and the same act. (Hence, the overt sexuality and aggression in Morris' recreations of the Middle Ages.)

Appropriately, the Sundering Flood—the central image in the romance—also has an historical significance. Rising in the mountains, it passes through various stages of civilization until reaching, at its mouth, the City of the Sundering Flood, where the king and merchants are engaged in a class struggle with the proletarian "Lesser Crafts." Osberne and Elfhind begin their lives in a proto-feudal society near the sources of the river. Osberne's military exploits—his attempt to find Elfhild—take him as far south as the City of the Sundering Flood, where he participates decisively in the victory of the working class. (There is even a replay of the Trafalgar Square Riot, in which the workers are victorious.) But Osberne does not choose to remain in the city. Despairing that he will ever find Elfhild, he determines to go back "to my fold in the Dale beside the Sundering Flood, and there . . . live and die in such content as I may" (XXI, 183). Just as he had earlier refused knighthood (XXI, 106), Osberne turns his back on historical progress and returns to a version of upper barbarism (that is, late gens society) epitomized by the communal life of Wethermel. In the beginning of the romance, the river was a fissure within this society. Significantly, it was the symbol of historical progress that obstructed the erotic fulfillment of the two lovers. Rejecting power (specifically, the power of a position in the feudal hierarchy), Osberne overcomes this obstacle and thus wins a victory over time itself.

In part owing to the sketchiness of its final episodes, *The Sundering Flood* does not offer a final solution to the questions that obsessed Morris during his last years. (In particular, the reunion of Osberne and Elfhild—in the midst of "The Wood Masterless"—fails to resolve all the issues raised by their separation.) Nevertheless, the romance's focus on Osberne's self-structures suggests Morris' growing insight into the workings of his own inner processes. What is striking, here and in the sequence of romances as a whole, is the steady evolution of his self-awareness. Piece by piece, Morris seems to have been constructing—and testing—a set of psychological paradigms with which to come to terms with the motivations (and inadequacies) underlying his life's work. And here, as throughout his development, one senses Morris feeling his way instinctively both toward an understanding of the central problems in his own personality and toward a representation of human experience with which he can rest satisfied in the fullness of his complete being.

CHAPTER 7

Conclusion

T HE instinctiveness that characterizes the evolving themes of the late romances is the hallmark of Morris' lifework. In design, it manifests itself as an instinctive grasp of the relationships of color to color, line to line. In politics, as an instinctive sense of the life struggling to express itself in social forms and as an instinctive contempt for the institutions and habits of mind that stand in the way of human fulfillment. ("A God who stands in the way of man making himself comfortable on the earth would be no God for me," he once wrote to William Allingham [*Letters*, 215].) And in his poetry and imaginative prose, it shows itself as an instinctive ability to submerge himself in a literary genre and work through it in such a way that its conventional themes and characters become the expression of his own deepest concerns.

Underlying Morris' success is a willingness to explore these concerns—not to prove a set of predetermined concepts, but to understand the sources of his own individual happiness. There is a disturbing strain of anti-intellectualism in *News from Nowhere*,[1] and Morris' self-avowed impatience with theoretical socialism has fostered the tradition that he was a man of feeling rather than of mind. But this is a misconception. Morris' intellect was simply rooted in firsthand experience. Theory followed—it did not precede—confrontation with the facts. He wrote about design on the basis of his experience as a designer; about manufacture on the basis of his experience working with his own hands. It follows that his characteristic weakness was the inability to understand what he had never himself undergone: thus, if he failed to grasp the longings of ordinary working men, it was because he had never known what it was like to work (for any length of time) for somebody else. And yet few men have confronted the facts as earnestly and as responsively as Morris. No other Victorian poet takes us closer to immediate states of human emotion than Morris. No Victorian novelist before Thomas Hardy is as frankly open in his treatment of sexuality as the author of *The Well at the World's End.*

Morris' uniqueness among the Victorians may account for the as yet incomplete rediscovery of his work in the twentieth century. He does not fit our customary generalizations about his period. Nor can he be reduced to a simple label. Pre-Raphaelite, craftsman, Marxist—he was all of these things, but the terms, either singly or taken as a group, fail to capture the essence of the man. George Bernard Shaw called him "a prophet and a saint" (*MM*, II, xxxix), and like other prophets and saints he challenges our complacencies. He demands that we take sides either with him or against him, and if his writings have been ignored it is in part because evasion was the safest way to ignore their challenge. Even E. P. Thompson's commanding study of Morris' evolution as a socialist (*William Morris: Romantic to Revolutionary*) went largely unnoticed when it was first published in 1955. And it has not been until the past decade that literary criticism has begun a significant reexamination of works like *The Earthly Paradise* and the late romances. There are, as yet, no modern editions of *Jason, The Earthly Paradise, Love is Enough,* or *Sigurd,* and Morris' reputation as a poet rests primarily on *The Defence of Guenevere* and a few bits and pieces of the later poetry. If books in print evidence a writer's current standing, our appreciation of Morris is as yet partial; his achievement as a poet, strikingly undervalued.

Illustrated catalogs of the work of Morris and Company and Kelmscott Press facsimiles suggest a growing interest in the aspect of Morris' career this study has perforce treated in least detail—his achievement as a designer. However, his accomplishments in this area are difficult to evaluate, and one must be careful to distinguish the influence of his theoretical writings from that of his actual practice. Placing Morris' wallpaper and chintz patterns in their historical context, Peter Floud has shown that they were far from revolutionary and that, generally speaking, the importance of Morris and Company was not the innovativeness or daring of its designs, but the high quality of their execution.[2] Morris reaffirmed the legitimacy of "the lesser arts" at a time when industrialization had all but given the deathblow to the traditional handicrafts and when the aesthetics of industrial design as yet offered little in their place. His alternative to the factory system and its shabby wares was a return to hand manufacture, and his example was a leading force behind the Arts and Crafts movement that flourished in England and the United States at the turn of the century.[3] Private presses sprang up on both sides of the Atlantic and turned out imitation Kelmscott Press books with heavy Gothic type and vellum bindings. Societies were founded and workshops established for the hand manufacture of solid, often clumsy, oak furniture and domestic implements in hand-forged metal and hand-blown glass. In some instances Morris' influence determined an entire lifework, as was the case with Elbert Hubbard. Hubbard met Morris in 1894 and, returning to East Aurora, New York, founded a press, then a bindery, then went into furniture making and metal work. His "Roycroft" became an artistic community, with an apprentice system and a cultural life not unrelated to that of Morris' Nowhere. But Morris' influence was most fruitful when it was the philosophy of his work, not his own particular tastes, that was accepted as a guide. His demonstration that a well-designed, well-produced book could be an object of high aesthetic value led to private press editions very different from the work of the Kelmscott Press, which in turn exerted a significant influence on later twentieth-century commercial typography. His concern for the beauty of day-to-day living played a role in the revitalization of domestic architecture and interior design that has taken place in our century.

The fundamental problem with Morris' theory of manufacture—and with the handicraft movement as a whole—was his refusal to perceive that machines could eliminate "useless toil" and at the same time produce objects of beauty. He did not foresee the ability of the machine to function as an extension of the artist's imagination and thus facilitate new, hitherto inaccessible forms. And yet, paradoxically, Morris' concern for functionalism and simplicity anticipates the ideals of the best twentieth-century machine design. Speaking in 1901 on "The Art and Craft of the Machine," Frank Lloyd Wright argued:

that he [Morris] miscalculated the machine does not matter. He did sublime work for it when he pleaded so well for the process of elimination its abuse had made necessary; when he fought the innate vulgarity of theocratic impulse in art as opposed to democratic; and when he preached the gospel of simplicity.

All artists love and honor William Morris.

He did the best in his time for art and will live in history as the great socialist, together with Ruskin, the great moralist.[4]

Wright in the United States and Walter Gropius in Germany—perhaps the two leading figures in modern architecture—regarded

Morris as a significant predecessor. Thus, his concern for the integrity of materials, for the organic relationship between form and function, and for simplicity provided an ideological basis for a school of design in many respects radically dissimilar to his own work.[5] Morris' medievalism has its twentieth-century counterpart in the apprentice system of Wright's Taliesin Fellowship and in Gropius' conception of the Bauhaus as "a new guild of crafts without the class distinction . . . a working community."[6] For both Wright and Gropius—as for Morris—the end of architecture is life itself: the architect does not merely design buildings, he designs their contents as well—tables, chairs, dishes, glassware—with a profound understanding of the specific human needs they must meet and fulfill.

Given Morris' concern for these human needs, it is appropriate that his contribution to socialism—over and above the example of his personal commitment to its cause—is the standard of life he offers as the criterion of a successful revolution. As E. P. Thompson has made clear, the important issue is not whether or not Morris was a "Marxist," but the nature of his contribution to what has come to be called "Marxism."[7] For Thompson, the greatness of Morris lies in his supplying the very element self-evidently missing in Marxism as it has come to be practiced in our century: "its lack of a moral self-consciousness or even a vocabulary of desire, its inability to project any images of the future, or even its tendency to fall back in lieu of these upon the Utilitarian's earthly paradise—the maximisation of economic growth."[8] So perceived, *News from Nowhere* and essays like "How We Live and How We Might Live" and "A Factory as It Might Be" are not merely critiques of capitalist society, but also of any communist society that cannot measure up to the level of human fulfillment Morris envisions. Whatever our economic philosophy, we ignore him at our peril.

This study has stressed Morris' career as a writer. I have argued that this aspect of his work can and should be treated as a self-defining whole. Yet it is also true that his poetry and imaginative prose are fully appreciated only in the context of his entire accomplishment in all fields. Like his socialism, like his work as a designer and craftsman, his development as a poet is a reflection of his search for a satisfactory way of life. The medievalism of his earlier prose and poetry is a challenge to industrial society; its psychosexual realism, to the morality we oversimplifyingly call "Victorian." More important, from a formalist perspective, his problems in finding a narrative voice reflected a discontent with the literary models current in his own century. As a poet and romancer, Morris rejected romantic subjectivism and sought in its place a voice rooted in literary and folk tradition: he sought to create a body of literature that was the expression not of one man but of the English people—not as they were but as they might become. In this respect, Morris' work can be read as a response to Matthew Arnold's call for a literature based on "the great primary human affections . . . those elementary feelings which subsist permanently in the race and are independent of time."[9] Yet Morris grasped what Arnold did not—the necessary relationship between folk art and more sophisticated literary forms.

Although they have always had their admirers—Yeats, who adopted their symbolism; C. S. Lewis and J. R. R. Tolkein, who adopted their genre—it has not been until the last decade that Morris' late romances (in which the relationship between folk art and sophisticated literature is most fully developed) have begun to reach the popular audience for which they were intended. The romances, including *News from Nowhere* and *A Dream of John Ball,* are among the first literary expressions of postindustrial society—of a society secure in its recognition of the physical needs of the human animal, a society concerned with the relationship between man and his environment, a society concerned with the problems of its own power. Changing tastes have distanced us from the narrative poetry for which Morris was best known by his contemporaries (*Jason* and *The Earthly Paradise*); nevertheless, he remains—one suspects he would be happy to know—a writer cherished by more than a narrow body of literary specialists.

Yet the achievement of William Morris is not to be measured by literary, artistic, or political influence—much less by the number of his books sold in the last decade. The man strikes us because he is terrifying. He speaks out with the impatient individualism of a precocious child. Like many precocious children, he never fully opened himself to human relationships. But his very aloofness—his refusal to accept the world as he found it—makes him a model for any of us who long to make the world a more adequate place for human life. To come to know Morris, whatever the avenue of approach, is to find him a "fact" of one's existence. He becomes, inescapably, a conscience.

Notes and References

Chapter One

1. *The Letters of William Morris to his Family and Friends,* ed. Philip Henderson (London: Longmans, Green, 1950), p. 184; hereafter cited as *Letters.*
2. J. W. Mackail, *The Life of William Morris* (1899; rpt. New York: Benjamin Blom, 1968), I, 9.
3. For a detailed argument on this matter, see Jack Lindsay, *William Morris: His Life and Work* (London: Constable, 1975), pp. 27–33.
4. Lindsay is the only biographer who has bothered to explain the Marlborough riots (see ibid., pp. 33–35).
5. Mackail, I, 17.
6. R. W. Dixon, quoted by Mackail, I, 52.
7. D. G. Rossetti, quoted by Mackail, I, 113.
8. Mackail, I, 143.
9. This and subsequent parenthetical references are to *The Collected Works of William Morris,* ed. May Morris, 24 vols. (1910–1915; rpt. New York: Russell and Russell, 1966).
10. This aborted scheme is the subject of Joseph R. Dunlap's *Book that Never Was* (New York: Oriole Editions, 1971).
11. May Morris, *William Morris: Artist, Writer, Socialist,* 2 vols. (1936; rpt. New York: Russell and Russell, 1966), II, 136; hereafter cited in the text as *MM.*
12. Quoted by E. P. Thompson, *William Morris: Romantic to Revolutionary,* 2d ed. (New York: Pantheon Books, 1977), p. 321.
13. Quoted in ibid., pp. 344–45.
14. For the history of this interest, see H. Halliday Sparling, *The Kelmscott Press and William Morris Master Craftsman* (1924; rpt. Folkestone, England: William Dawson, 1975).

Chapter Two

1. For a more detailed support of this interpretation, see my "Morris' 'Childe Roland': The Deformed not quite Transformed," *The Pre-Raphaelite Review,* 1 (1977), 95–105.
2. See Peter Faulkner, ed., *William Morris: The Critical Heritage* (London: Routledge and Kegan Paul, 1973), pp. 32–37, 40–42.
3. *The Critical Heritage,* pp. 31, 42–45.

4. Lindsay is particularly vocal in his defence of this aspect of the poems (see pp. 98f.).

5. *The Critical Heritage*, pp. 33–34.

6. For a bibliography of this criticism, see Dennis R. Balch, "Guenevere's Fidelity to Arthur in 'The Defense of Guenevere' and 'King Arthur's Tomb,' " *Victorian Poetry*, 13, nos. 3–4 (Fall–Winter 1975), 61n.

7. See ibid., 62–66.

8. The uncertain antecedent of *this* (line 8 in the extract) is a good example of Guenevere's syntactic ambiguity. Her preference for semicolons is more subtly misleading.

9. Mackail, I, 45.

10. For a specific account of Morris' indebtedness to Froissart, see John Patrick, "Morris and Froissart: 'Geffray Teste Noire' and 'The Haystack in the Floods,' " *Notes and Queries*, 5 (October 1958), 425–27; "Morris and Froissart Again: 'Sir Peter Harpdon's End,' " *Notes and Queries*, 6 (September 1959), 331–33.

11. Dianne F. Sadoff, "Erotic Murders: Structural and Rhetorical Irony in William Morris' Froissart Poems," *Victorian Poetry*, 13, nos. 3–4 (Fall–Winter 1975), 18. (I am indebted to a number of the critical insights in this important article.)

12. Mackail calls them "poems of a wholly unbased and fantastic romance" (I, 133); in his edition of the *Early Romances in Prose and Verse* (London: J. M. Dent, 1973), Peter Faulkner labels them "The Poems of Fantasy" and observes that "they point forward in time . . . to the aesthetic movement and *art nouveau*" (XV–XVI).

13. Robert L. Stallman, " 'Rapunzel' Unravelled," *Victorian Poetry*, 7 (1969), 227.

14. "Imaginative Transformation in William Morris' 'Rapunzel,' " *Victorian Poetry*, 12 (1974), 153–164.

Chapter Three

1. See Blue Calhoun, *The Pastoral Vision of William Morris* (Athens: University of Georgia Press, 1975), pp. 61–87.

2. Ibid., p. 102.

3. According to Carole Silver, "Morris visualized the Wanderers' voyage as an unrecorded Norse exploration of the New World" ("*The Earthly Paradise*: Lost," *Victorian Poetry*, 13, nos. 3–4 [Fall–Winter 1975], 29).

4. Morris' contribution to the legend is the route by which the Argonauts return from Aea to Greece—"probably . . . north by the Don or the Dvina and . . . out by the Vistula," as he explained his unorthodox geography (II, XXIV), to the Baltic sea; thence around the western coast of Europe, through the Straits of Gibraltar and home.

5. "*The Earthly Paradise*: Lost," 31.

6. Ibid., p. 34.

7. Calhoun's discussion of this element in the story is particularly good (p. 165).

8. "A Defence of Poetry," in *Shelley's Prose*, ed. David Lee Clark (Alburquerque: University of New Mexico Press, 1954), p. 294.

Chapter Four

1. I have resisted identifying Morris with "Aestheticism"—despite Walter Pater's decision to reprint his review of *The Earthly Paradise* with the title "Aesthetic Poetry" in the first edition of *Appreciations* (1889). Morris was never a proponent of art for art's sake, and with his growing estrangement from Rossetti, he became increasingly hostile to the theory of art he advocated.

2. For an expanded form of the following argument, see my "Travel as Autobiography: William Morris' *Icelandic Journals*," in *Approaches to Victorian Autobiography*, ed. George Landow (Athens, Ohio: Ohio University Press, 1979).

3. This section summarizes my earlier "*Love is Enough:* A Crisis in William Morris' Poetic Development," *Victorian Poetry*, 15 (Winter 1977), 297–306.

4. Among the letters included in the appendix to the first edition of E. P. Thompson's *William Morris: Romantic to Revolutionary* (New York: Monthly Review Press, 1961), p. 879. (This appendix is omitted from the 1977 edition cited elsewhere in this study.)

5. "The Victorian Skald: Old Icelandic and the Evolution of William Morris' *Sigurd the Volsung*," Special Session: William Morris' *Sigurd the Volsung, 1876–1976*, MLA Convention, New York, 27 December 1976.

6. Northrop Frye, *Fearful Symmetry: A Study of William Blake* (Boston: Beacon Press, 1962), p. 316.

7. Robert W. Gutman discusses Morris' treatment of his sources in detail in his introduction to *Volsunga Saga: The Story of the Volsungs and Niblungs*, trans. William Morris (New York: Collier Books, 1962).

8. See Karl Litzenberg, "The Social Philosophy of William Morris and the Doom of the Gods," in *Essays and Studies in English and Comparative Literature*, University of Michigan Publications 1 (1933), 183–203.

9. E. O. G. Turville-Petre, *Myth and Religion of the North: The Religion of Ancient Scandinavia* (New York: Holt, Rinehart and Winston, 1964), p. 111.

Chapter Five

1. As Graham Hough argues in *The Last Romantics* (New York: Barnes and Noble, 1961), p. 97.

2. "William Morris and the Dream of Revolution", in *Literature and Politics in the Nineteenth Century,* ed. John Lucas (London: Metheun and Company, 1971), p. 254.

3. Morris did not read German, and Engels' study was not translated into English until after his death.

4. *Ancient Society, or Researches in the Lines of Human Progress from Savagery through Barbarism to Civilization* (London: Macmillan, 1877).

5. *The Origin of the Family, Private Property and the State,* ed. Eleanor Burke Leacock (New York: International Publishers, 1975), p. 237.

6. Goode, p. 269.

Chapter Six

1. Jack Lindsay argues this interpretation (pp. 344–45).

2. Ibid., p. 344.

3. In a provocative essay on "The Erotic in *News from Nowhere* and *The Well at the World's End,*" Norman Kelvin speculates on the "fantasies of sadistic male power" that characterize Ralph's relationships with the women in his life (*Studies in the Late Romances of William Morris* [New York: William Morris Society, 1976], p. 107).

Chapter Seven

1. Discussed by Lionel Trilling in "Agression and Utopia, A Note on William Morris's 'News from Nowhere,' " *Psychoanalytic Quarterly,* 42 (1973), 214–25.

2. See "The Inconstencies of William Morris," *Listener,* 52 (1954), 615–17; "William Morris as an Artist: A New View," *Listener,* 52 (1954), 562–64.

3. For an account of the Arts and Crafts movement in the United States, see Robert Judson Clark, ed., *The Arts and Crafts Movement in America 1876–1916* (Princeton, N.J.: Princeton University Press, 1972).

4. *Frank Lloyd Wright: Writings and Buildings,* ed. Edgar Kaufmann and Ben Raeburn (Horizon Press, 1960), p. 56.

5. Although Wright contrasts himself with Morris on the issue of machine design, his account of building Taliesin from native materials with local workmen and of its relationship to its setting sounds very much like Morris' description of Kelmscott Manor (compare "Gossip about an Old House on the Upper Thames," *MM,* I, 364–71, with "Taliesin," in *Writings and Buildings,* 172–181).

6. Quoted by Charles Jencks, *Modern Movements in Architecture* (Garden City: Doubleday, 1973), p. 59. See also Nikolaus Pevsner, *Pioneers of Modern Design from William Morris to Walter Gropius* (New York: Museum of Modern Art, 1949).

7. Thompson, p. 807.

8. Ibid., p. 792.

9. "Preface to *Poems*, 1853," in *The Portable Matthew Arnold*, ed. Lionel Trilling (New York: Viking, 1949), p. 188.

Selected Bibliography

PRIMARY SOURCES

The Collected Works of William Morris. Edited by May Morris. 24 vols. London: Longmans, Green, 1910-1915; rpt. New York: Russell and Russell, 1966.
The Letters of William Morris to His Family and Friends. Edited by Philip Henderson. London: Longmans, Green, 1950.
The Story of Kormak the Son of Ogmund. Edited by Grace J. Calder. London: William Morris Society, 1970.
The Unpublished Lectures of William Morris. Edited by Eugene D. LeMire. Detroit: Wayne State University Press, 1969.
William Morris: Artist, Writer, Socialist. Edited by May Morris. 2 vols. Oxford: Blackwells, 1936; rpt. New York: Russell and Russell, 1966.

SECONDARY SOURCES

ARNOT, R. PAGE. *William Morris: The Man and the Myth, Including Letters of William Morris to J. L. Mahon and Dr. John Glasse.* New York: Monthly Review Press, 1964. A short, polemical account of Morris' development as a socialist.
BLOOM, HAROLD. *Yeats.* New York: Oxford University Press, 1970. Treats Morris' influence on Yeats.
BRANTLINGER, PATRICK. " 'News from Nowhere': Morris's Socialist Anti-Novel." *Victorian Studies,* 19 (1975), 35–50. Among the best recent interpretations of *News from Nowhere.*
BRYSON, JOHN, ed. *Dante Gabriel Rossetti and Jane Morris: Their Correspondence.* Oxford: Oxford University Press, 1976. Most of the letters are Rossetti's and reveal more about him than her.
BURNE-JONES, GEORGIANA. *Memorials of Edward Burne-Jones.* New York: Macmillan, 1906. Reminiscences of Morris by one of the few persons with whom he had a close relationship.
CALHOUN, BLUE. *The Pastoral Vision of William Morris.* Athens, Ga.: University of Georgia Press, 1975. Major criticism of *The Earthly Paradise.*
———— et al. *Studies in the Late Romances of William Morris.* New York: William Morris Society, 1976. Useful essays on the late romances. (Subsequent volumes in this series will collect papers on *Sigurd the Volsung* and Morris' early poetry and prose.)

CLARK, FIONA. *William Morris: Wallpapers and Chintzes.* 2d ed. London: Academy Editions, 1974. An illustrated catalog of Morris and Company's work.

COMPTON-RICKETT, ARTHUR. *William Morris: A Study in Personality.* London: H. Jenkins, 1913. Firsthand anecdotes.

CROW, GERALD H. *William Morris Designer.* London: Studio, 1934. An illustrated survey of Morris' career as a designer.

DUNLAP, JOSEPH. *The Book That Never Was.* New York: Oriole Editions, 1971. Treats Morris and Burne-Jones' abortive attempt to publish *The Earthly Paradise* as a decorated book.

ESHLEMAN, LLOYD W. *A Victorian Rebel: The Life of William Morris.* New York: Charles Scribner's, 1940. Reissued as *William Morris: Prophet of England's New Order* by Lloyd Eric Grey (London: Cassell, 1949). An untrustworthy account of Morris' political philosophy.

EVANS, B. IFOR. *William Morris and His Poetry.* London: George G. Harrap, 1925. Too brief to be of much use.

FAULKNER, PETER, ed. *William Morris, The Critical Heritage.* London: Routledge and Kegan Paul, 1973. Contemporary reviews and criticism of Morris' literary work.

FREDEMAN, WILLIAM E., ed. *Victorian Poetry: An Issue Dedicated to the Work of William Morris,* 13, nos. 3–4 (Fall–Winter 1975). A collection of recent criticism on various aspects of Morris' work.

FLOUD, PETER. "The Inconsistencies of William Morris." *Listener,* 52 (1954), 562–64. Placing Morris' designs in their historical context, argues his work was characterized by high quality rather than originality.

GARDNER, DELBERT R. *An "Idle Singer" and His Audience: A Study of William Morris's Poetic Reputation in England, 1858–1900.* The Hague: Mouton, 1975.

GLASIER, J. BRUCE. *William Morris and the Early Days of the Socialist Movement.* London: Longmans, Green, 1921. Firsthand, but unreliable. (Glasier attempt to make Morris over in his own image.)

GOODE, JOHN. "William Morris and the Dream of Revolution." In *Literature and Politics in the Nineteenth Century,* edited by John Lucas. New York: Barnes and Noble, 1971. An important Marxist explication of Morris' Socialist romances.

HENDERSON, PHILIP. *William Morris, His Life, Work and Friends.* New York: McGraw-Hill, 1967. The first biography to treat "the facts" of Morris' marriage. Unfortunately, a pedestrian account of his work.

HOARE, DOROTHY M. *The Works of Morris and Yeats in Relation to Early Saga Literature.* New York: Macmillan, 1937. Arrogant and foolish.

HOUGH, GRAHAM. "William Morris." In *The Last Romantics.* New York: Barnes and Noble, 1961. A twentieth-century revaluation of Morris' work.

KIRCHHOFF, FREDERICK. "*Love is Enough:* A Crisis in William Morris' Poetic Development." *Victorian Poetry*, 15 (1977), 297–306.

KOCMANOVÁ, JESSE. *The Poetic Maturing of William Morris*. New York: Folcroft Library, 1970. A Marxist treatment of Morris' development. Occasionally insightful.

LEBOURGEOIS, J. Y. "William Morris and the Marxist Myth." *Durham University Journal* (December 1976), 76-82. An unsuccessful attempt to refute E. P. Thompson's interpretation of Morris' Marxism.

LEWIS, C. S. "William Morris." In *Rehabilitations and Other Essays*. London: Oxford Univeristy Press, 1939. An assessment of Morris by a twentieth-century writer strongly influenced by his work.

LINDSAY, JACK. *William Morris: His Life and Work*. London: Constable, 1975. The most recent biography of Morris. Useful, but far from definitive.

LITZENBERG, KARL. "The Social Philosphy of William Morris and the Doom of the Gods." In *Essays and Studies in English and Comparative Literature*. University of Michigan Publications 1 (1933), 183–203. Relates Morris' revolutionary socialism to the concept of Ragnarök.

―――. "William Morris and Scandinavian Literature: A Bibliographical Essay." *Scandinavian Studies and Notes*, 13 (1935), 93–105. A useful bibliographical essay.

MACKAIL, J. W. *The Life of William Morris*. 1899; rpt. New York: Benjamin Blom, 1968. The standard biography. (Mackail was Burne-Jones' son-in-law.) An indispensible source, but biased against Morris' radical socialism.

MACLEOD, ROBERT DUNCAN. *Morris Without Mackail, As Seen by His Contemporaries*. Glasgow: W. and R. Holmes, 1954.

MAURER, OSCAR. "William Morris and the Poetry of Escape." In *Nineteenth-Century Studies*, edited by Herbert Davis et al., 1940; rpt. New York: Greenwood Press, 1968 pp. 247–76. Argues Morris' popularity with victorian readers was largely a response to the escapism of his early poetry.

MEIER, PAUL. *Le Pensée Utopique de William Morris*. Paris: Editions Sociaies, 1972. Prolix and unnecessary attempt to "prove" Morris a Marxist.

MORTON, A. L. *The English Utopia*. London: Lawrence and Wishart, 1953. Contains a chapter on *News from Nowhere*.

NEEDHAM, PAUL et al. *William Morris and the Art of the Book*. New York: Oxford University Press, 1976. Essays on Morris as a typographer, orthographer, and bibliophile.

SADOFF, DIANNE F. "Imaginative Transformation in William Morris' 'Rapunzel.' " *Victorian Poetry*, 12 (1974), 153–64. A provocative psychological reading of the poem.

SEWTER, A. C. *The Stained Glass of William Morris and His Circle*. New Haven: Yale University Press, 1974. Richly illustrated.

SILVER, CAROLE. " 'The Defence of Guenevere': A Further Interpretation."

Studies in English Literature, 9 (1969), 695–702. Examines the rhetorical strategy of Morris' poem in light of recent criticism.

SPARLING, HENRY HALLIDAY. *The Kelmscott Press and William Morris Master-Craftsman.* 1924; rpt. Folkestone, England: William Dawson, 1975. A firsthand account of Morris and the Kelmscott Press.

THOMPSON, E. P. *William Morris: Romantic to Revolutionary.* 2d ed. New York: Pantheon Books, 1977. Traces Morris' development as a socialist in great detail. The most significant study of Morris yet written.

THOMPSON, PAUL. *The Work of William Morris.* New York: Viking Press, 1967. A good survey of Morris' work in various fields. Weakest in dealing with his literary development.

WATKINSON, RAY. *William Morris as Designer.* New York: Reinhold Publishing Corp., 1967. A general survey of Morris' work as a designer. Superficial.

YEATS, WILLIAM BUTLER. "The Happiest of Poets." In *Ideas of Good and Evil: Essays and Introductions.* New York: Macmillan, 1961. An appreciation of Morris by a major twentieth-century poet whose work he strongly influenced.

Index